Lost China

Lost China

The Photographs of Leone Nani

SKIRA

PIME
dal 1850

Art Director
Marcello Francone

Editing
Emanuela Di Lallo

Layout
Serena Parini

Translations
Rhoda Billingsley
Adrian Hartley Cook

First published in Italy in 2003
by Skira Editore S.p.A.
Palazzo Casati Stampa
via Torino 61
20123 Milano
Italy
www.skira.net

Printed and bound in Italy. First edition

ISBN 88-8491-571-6

Distributed in North America and Latin
America by Rizzoli International
Publications, Inc. through St. Martin's
Press, 175 Fifth Avenue, New York,
NY 10010.
Distributed elsewhere in the world
by Thames and Hudson Ltd., 181a
High Holborn, London WC1V 7QX,
United Kingdom.

Edited by
Clara Bulfoni and Anna Pozzi

*This book has been published according
to the will of*

Centro missionario PIME, Milan
Father Vincenzo Pavan, Director

Museo Popoli e Culture, PIME, Milan
Father Massimo Casaro, Director

With the support of
Italo-Chinese Institute
Mondo e missione magazine

We wish to express our deepest gratitude to
Father Mario Marazzi
Father Dino Doimo
Lara Fornasini
Andrea Ferrari
Bruno Maggi
Giulia Mattace
Mauro Moret

Authors of the essays
Fulvio De Giorgi
*Professor of Contemporary History,
Università Cattolica di Brescia*

Sergio Ticozzi
PIME missionary, China specialist

Federico Masini
*Professor of Chinese Language
and Literature, Università di Roma
'La Sapienza'*

Roberto Festorazzi
Journalist and historian

Lionello Lanciotti
*Professor Emeritus of Chinese Philology,
Università degli Studi di Napoli
'L'Orientale'*

Giovanna Calvenzi
Photo-editor

Introductions to the photographic
sections of this book are edited
by Clara Bulfoni (*c.b.*).

The photographs by Father Leone Nani
are preserved in the PIME Archives,
Milan.
All the rights of the photos' reproduction
are the property of Pimedit onlus, Milan,
and are reserved for all countries.

Foreword

The nineteenth and twentieth centuries were crowded with dramatic events in China. Then, just as it is today, the huge empire was a focus of interest for the West, and they were interests with their roots buried deep in the Augustan age. There were instances of trade with the Roman Empire where the fragrant spices and precious silks of China were keenly sought after.

Contacts were resumed in the 13th century after a silence of some eight centuries, interrupted only by occasional trading among merchants and caravans, thanks to the evangelical spirit of the Catholic Church when a vain attempt was made to convert the Mongol emperors.

The first to reach China at this stage were the Venetians Niccolò and Matteo Polo between 1260 and 1269. Their subsequent expedition was joined by the young Marco Polo who succeeded in coming into close contact with the Chinese civilisation and whose memoirs, Il Milione, were written for posterity.

Father Leone Nani appeared much like a new Marco Polo when he arrived in China at the age of 23 in the first years of the twentieth century. Enthused by his reception by the Chinese people he was able to capture, in his photographs, the disappearing spirit of a people overwhelmed by events which were to devastate their millennial soul.

The final years of the nineteenth century and the first of the twentieth were among the hardest China had to endure in its long history of civil conflicts and foreign aggression. The year 1842 marked the beginning of a decline that proved impossible to halt, the Western powers wresting important concessions from China by the force of their military ascendancy. The wars that followed—all of them lost—were hopeless struggles against Russia, then Japan and the Boxer rebellion of 1900. The fall of the Qing dynasty in 1911 had become inevitable.

This was the China Father Nani succeeded in capturing, an empire sliding downhill to disintegration. At the same time, however, it was creating the foundations whence it could rise from the ashes; a nation in the process of formation was passing through the long and painful phases of rebirth.

Father Nani's photographs are images of a precious past, the memory of a vanished China. Thanks to this book it lives again, in pages that shed light on sentiments that inspired the missionary in his discovery of 'his' China. The photographs are fleeting portraits of a daily life remote to us, but in them we perceive his curiosity and the deep respect he had for this culture and this people.

Father Nani's life in China, his attitude towards such a radically different and traditionalist reality, is beyond doubt a lesson for our times. The tolerance revealed in his work is synonymous with respect for a culture whose values were not his own, and whose customs were foreign.

So it is a great honour for me to present this volume and its precious contents which not only enclose traces of a distant past, but also carry a message for our own day.

Cesare Romiti
President of the Italo-Chinese Institute

Contents

Introduction

Giancarlo Politi

Many were the missionaries in the history of the PIME (Pontificio Istituto Missioni Estere, or Pontifical Institute for Foreign Missions) who, at the same time they were evangelising and trying to improve living conditions, devoted themselves to the study and investigation of the socio-cultural context of the countries in which they lived. Famous among them were Father Carlo Salerio (1827–70), a missionary in Oceania and a passionate anthropologist; Monsignor Simeone Volontieri (1831–1904), the apostolic vicar of the Chinese province of Henan and an expert cartographer who compiled and had printed a map of the colony of Hong Kong that was for long considered the best one available and was adopted by the British authorities themselves; or Father Raffaello Maglioni (1891–1953), a missionary in Hong Kong who brought to light a great quantity of finds from the Neolithic cultures of southern China.

It is with that same missionary spirit and interest in other cultures and religions that the Institute is present in fifteen countries today throughout the world, especially in Asia, a continent for which the PIME has always reserved particular attention.

And very special indeed was the attention that another missionary of the PIME, Father Leone Nani, had for China, in particular for the region of Shaanxi, where he was sent in the early part of the nineteenth century. Today we are rediscovering his work through the publication of many of his extraordinary photographs that bear witness not only to the singular personality of that generous and enterprising missionary, but also to a world that has disappeared, a way of life he immortalised in photographs of great eloquence and evocativeness.

Father Nani left Albino (near Bergamo), where he was born in 1880, in September 1903, a little more than three months after he had been ordained a priest. His destination was the city of Hanzhong, located in a luxuriant valley secluded in the southern mountains of the Chinese province of Shaanxi. The Catholic mission extended over the Qin Ling mountain chain and had its centre at Guluba, not far from the city of the same name. Reminiscent of the Italian Alps, the mountains are steep and wild, and cut by the deep scars left by impetuous rivers. One of these is the Han which rises here and crosses through the entire region from west to east and also gives its name to the prevalent ethnic group in China; another is the vorticose Jialing Jiang which borders on the west with the Gansu and continues through the gorges of Sichuan, seeking the majestic Chang Jiang (or Yangtze) which it joins at Chongqing. Rivers constitute the wealth of these lands as well as their ruin, because of the frequent, devastating floods. For centuries they were the most important and almost only means of communication with the rest of China. However, efficient means of communication were meant to serve the State bureaucracy, not trade or cultural exchanges. The population, living in a subsistence economy, had always been subject to the whims and duplicity of government administrators. A quick form of 'justice' functioned as a formidable instrument of control, but proved ineffective when used to suppress popular incentives demanding a fairer distribution of the wealth. Much blood was shed in these lands during the nineteenth century, most of it in vain.

About a quarter of a century before Leone Nani's arrival, the Pope sent out a small group of missionaries who belonged to the Seminario per le Estere Missioni dei Santi Apostoli Pietro e Paolo (Seminary for the Foreign Mission of the Apostolic Saints Peter and Paul), which had been founded in Rome in 1871. In Milan, an analogous Seminary for the Foreign Missions had already been operating for some twenty years since its foundation in 1850. In 1926, the two seminaries joined forces to form the PIME.

Between 1876 (the year of the departure of the first apostolic vicar, Monsignor Gregorio Antonucci) and 1902, twenty-one of these 'adventurers', in eleven small groups, reached those mountains. Seven died prematurely, struck down by the damp, unhealthy climate. One of them, Alberico Crescitelli, was killed in July 1900 during the Boxer Rebellion in which more than thirty thousand Christians lost their lives in just a few weeks. Others were forced to return home for reasons of health. Like a seed tossed into the great sea of the more than five million

people dwelling in those valleys, the small Christian community owed its birth and growth to those missionaries. That population still lives in conditions of poverty and hardship.

I returned for the second time to Hanzhong in 1988, together with two veteran missionaries of that area, who had begun their ministry in those mountains in the late 1940s only to be expelled a few years later by the new regime. When faced with the misery and desperation that continues to afflict the lives of so many in that area, one of them fell into a distressing and profound silence.

But the seed tossed by these and other missionaries who went before them continues to grow luxuriantly in spite of adversities; at times it is bent by a contrary and violent wind, and it is often heavily trod upon, but it has neither been beaten down nor uprooted.

During Nani's days, as well as in the subsequent decades, the missionaries were required to travel continually from one community to the other, covering long distances on foot or on the back of a mule as they followed the paths on the mountain ridges surrounding the valley. They were often forced to absent themselves from their homes for long periods, and more often than not were without basic comforts.

However, there were also advantages to that way of life. Father Leone had all the time he wanted to admire the breathtakingly beautiful landscapes, and to impress the hundreds of faces of

the people he met on his memory and in his heart. Only
afterwards were these masterfully committed to the camera,
with every tiny detail recorded and treasured. At times, there
was even a touch of humour, especially in his self-portraits.
And it is this aspect in particular—as well as the beauty of his
photographs—that, in my opinion, motivates the PIME to
remember this man after so many years: the way he approached
his fellow man with veneration and respect without ever being
banal, his ability to grasp in each and everyone the struggle to
live and the love of existence and beauty. Nani's lens captured
this man, the object of great respect, deeming him worthy of
hope, ready to welcome and preserve in his heart the beauty
therein.

Nani had a passion for faces and as he photographed
—probably unwittingly—he committed to posterity a world
that was about to disappear forever.

Perhaps because—but he never said this—he was seeking a Face
(Psalm 27,8) that he knew was always hidden (Psalm 13,1) in
the lives of men. And with his exacting camera he sang praises
to Him for whom he had come to the valley of Hanzhong.
A silent praise transmitted down to us, one which became an
insistent entreaty for *that* Face to shine with tenderness and
love on the life of the people he was meeting those days.

The History

Nani's Italy

Fulvio De Giorgi

Leone Nani was born in Albino, near Bergamo, on 19 August 1880, and he departed for China in 1903. His 'Italian' formation took place therefore between the last two decades of the nineteenth century and the first three years of the twentieth century. But what exactly was Nani's Italy? Or rather: was there one single Italy then? From a politico-institutional point of view, the unification of Italy occurred in 1861 and ended in 1870 with the conquest of Rome the capital. Nani was born only ten years after this final symbolic event of the Risorgimento, at which time most of its protagonists had disappeared from the scene. In 1878, two of the leading ones, Pope Pius IX and King Victor Emmanuel II died. The conclave elected as pope Gioacchino Pecci, who took the name of Leo XIII. At the same time, Umberto I ascended to the throne, inaugurating what would be called the 'Umbertine era': a period that witnessed not only the birth of the Socialist Party in 1881, but also Crispi's authoritarianism which was marked by Italy's unsuccessful imperialist attempt in Africa as well as the increased social agitation leading up to the dramatic events at the end of the century in 1898 (the year in which Nani arrived in Rome) and the assassination of the king in Monza in 1900.

In the world of culture, positivism was the prevailing force. In the year of Nani's birth, Aristide Gabelli, an outstanding exponent of Italian pedagogical positivism, published *Il metodo d'insegnamento nelle scuole elementari d'Italia* (Teaching method in the elementary schools of Italy) and Cesare Lombroso founded the *Archivio di psichiatria, scienze penali e antropologia criminale* (Archive of psychiatry, penal sciences and criminal anthropology).

But this Umbertine, secular,[1] liberal and positivist Italy was not really Nani's Italy. His was the Catholic Italy, the Italy of the Pope, the Italy of Leo XIII. It therefore comes as no surprise that his parents named him after the new pope, at a time when not only the 'Roman question' was still very pertinent and the Pope considered a 'prisoner in the Vatican', but when there was also a growing and deep-felt devotion for the Roman Pontiff among the Catholic population. Within the Nani family (one of his brothers, Attilio, also became a priest), these feelings must have been cultivated in a simple way; they would later be developed in the sense of a militant Catholic intransigence in the archiepiscopal seminary of Bergamo where young Leone Nani studied until 1898. On the other hand, the bitter contrast between the Italian government, presided by Francesco Crispi, and the Pope following the inauguration of the monument to Giordano Bruno in the Roman square of Campo de' Fiori in June 1889 had had an enormous and long-lasting echo in the Italian Catholic world.

In the year of Leone Nani's birth, Leo XIII signed one of his most important documents regarding the missions, the *Sancta Dei Civitas*. In it, he denounced the damage inflicted on the missions by the secularism and anticlericalism of Catholic countries (like Italy or France): 'Indeed, we see the religious families, from which many have departed for holy missions, dissolved by hostile laws, the priests torn from their altars and forced to do military service, the property of one after another priest almost everywhere confiscated and proscribed'.[2] Then, in 1886, the Holy See sought to make an agreement with China for the exchange of diplomatic representatives, which, however, did not materialise—much to the disappointment of Pope Pecci—due to the strong protest of the French in the name of the French Republic's right to protect the Catholics in the Chinese territory (a 'patronage' conceded to France by the Tian Jin agreements of 1858).[3]

It was in this spiritual environment, marked by the struggle with secularism and by the defence of the Roman Pontiff, that Nani's choice to become a missionary matured and led him, not by chance, to Rome and the Pontificio Seminario dei Santi Apostoli Pietro e Paolo (Pontifical Seminary of the Holy Apostles Peter and Paul) or the Roman Mastai Seminary for Foreign Missions, founded under Pius IX (in 1926, it would unite with the Lombard Seminary for Foreign Missions to create the PIME). Emblematically, the dates seem to indicate Nani's closeness and that of his ambience to the intransigent culture. It is not surprising that his departure from Marseille for the Shaanxi vicariate in 1903 took place—it seems—on the symbolic date of anti-clerical secularism and the Italian Free Masonry—September 20, the anniversary of the breach of Porta Pia, the fall of papal Rome, and the end of papal temporal power. Nani evidently chose that date not so much because of a 'militant' contrast with the Masonic festivities but perhaps because of a spirit of expiation and reparation, according to the modulations of the intransigent spirituality of the times. Even the date of his promise in the Institute was meaningful: it occurred in fact in 1900 on the day of the Feast of the Immaculate Conception (the dogma proclaimed by Pius IX in 1854).

Nani's Italy was therefore the Italy of Leo XIII, the Leonine Italy: and he, born—as has been seen—two years after Pope Pecci's election, left the peninsula the same year as the Pope's death. The entire period of his formation in Italy prior to his departure for China took place therefore under the sign of the pastoral, spiritual and cultural policies of Leo XIII.

In the period of his formation at the Bergamo seminary, Nani distinguished himself in scientific studies (in which he obtained the highest marks). It was, moreover, a time in which, in line with the intellectual commitment encouraged by the Pope, the Italian ecclesiastical world in general, and the Lombard one in particular, showed a great interest in the sciences. There was in Lombardy a certain tradition of ecclesiastical 'naturalists', from the biologist Lazzaro Spallanzani to the geologist Antonio Stoppani. The bishop of Pavia, Agostino Riboldi, who had taught scientific subjects for years in the seminaries of Monza and Milan, was a student of mathematics and science, the author of a successful manual of physics, and, since 1895, an active member of the Italian Society of Natural Sciences. And it was Riboldi who, in 1880, entrusted the teaching of physics and natural history in the Pavia seminary to Don Pietro Maffi, who maintained it until 1901. Maffi, an eminent scientist, a student of astronomy and meteorology, a future cardinal and archbishop of Pisa, assumed a central role in those years, primarily through a series of publications: his articles in the Ambrosian journal *La Scuola Cattolica* (The Catholic School) aimed at the scientific updating of the seminary teachers. His vision, which must have had a certain influence, was also expressed in the 1898 book *Riflessioni sui nostri doveri davanti alla scienza e alla fede* (Reflections on our duties towards science and faith) and can be summarised as follows: 'Substantially, his thought consisted of three basic points: the importance of a cultural formation among the clergy even in the fields of the exact and natural sciences where the clash with non-believing scientists was all the more risky and bitter; a bold protest against the false and unjust transpositions that naturalists carried out from the point of view of observation to that of philosophy and the faith; the necessity—epistemological as well—to bring God back into science, or, in any case, the right of a scientist to also be a believer, rejecting the affirmation that faith might be detrimental to scientific seriousness and freedom'.[4]

Furthermore, during those same years, the last of the nineteenth century and the first of the twentieth, there was a rapid succession of important scientific discoveries and technical inventions: in 1895, the X-rays with Röntgen and the cinema with the Lumière brothers; in 1896, the radioactivity of uranium salts with Becquerel; in 1897, wireless telegraphy with Marconi; in 1898, radium with the Curies; in 1900, the quantum theory with Planck; in 1903, the first aeroplane flight of the Wright brothers. All of this provoked technological repercussions that profoundly changed daily life; one example was the diffusion of electric lights which began with the carbon filament lamp that Edison presented at the Universal Exposition of Paris in 1881 and witnessed so many improvements[5] thereafter, up to, in particular, the electric lighting of churches in the early twentieth century.[6]

The scientific and technical divulgation that involved much of the Italian middle class, conquered by the self-help myth,[7] made the fortunes of publishing houses like the Lombard Hoepli with its famous manuals that were republished so often between the nineteenth and twentieth centuries. One need only recall *Impianti di illuminazione elettrica* by the engineer Emilio Piazzoli, *Le Arti grafiche fotomeccaniche ossia la Eliografia nelle diverse applicazioni (Fotozincotipia, fotozincografia, fotolitografia, fotocollografia, fotosilografia, sincromia, ecc.)*, and *La Fotocromatografia* by L. Sassi (author also of *Le Proiezioni, Carte fotografiche. Preparazione e trattamento* as well as a *Ricettario fotografico*), *La Fotografia industriale* of Luigi Gioppi (who had also written a *Dizionario fotografico pei dilettanti e professionisti*), *Fotografia ortocromatica* by D. Bonacini, *Fotografia pei dilettanti* by G. Muffone, *Processi fotomeccanici* by Professor R. Namias (the author also of *Chimica fotografica*). All of these publications, moreover, give an idea of the rampant mania for photography in Italy those years.[8]

When Nani arrived in Rome, Pope Pecci had, of course, given a great impulse to the Catholic missions and the *implantatio Ecclesiae*; at that time, in fact, he had already established on the five continents 30 new Apostolic Prefectures, 49 Apostolic Vicariates and 11 Apostolic Vicariates from already existing Prefectures, 2 Apostolic Delegations, 2 new *Nullius Dioceseos* Abbacies, 100 new Dioceses, 17 Archiepiscopal Dioceses from already existing dioceses, 13 new Archiepiscopal Dioceses and 2 new Patriarchal Dioceses.[9]

But in Rome, where the Specola Vaticana had been founded among other things in 1891, a specific measure on the part of the Catholic scientific movement began to develop at an international level, thanks also to papal stimulus. No longer was it only due to some pioneering magazines that were read in Italy (for example by Maffi)—like the *Revue des questions scientifiques*, founded in 1877 by the Jesuit Ignazio Carbonelle as an expression of the Scientific Society of Brussels, or the Parisian *Cosmos*, promoted by the Abbot Francesco Moigno—but rather to the movement of the International Congresses of Catholic Scientists[10] that took place every three years between 1888 and 1900. The first (1888)[11] and the second (1891) were held in Paris, the third (1894) in Brussels,[12] the fourth at Fribourg in Switzerland (1897)[13] with the participation—among others—of Achille Ratti[14] (the future Pope Pius XI), and the fifth in Munich (1900).[15]

Animating this movement were some important French Catholics: Monsignor Maurice d'Hulst,[16] rector of the Catholic Institute of Paris, Canon Duilhé de Saint-Projet and the geologist Albert de Lapparent.[17] The Italian Catholic Society for Scientific Studies was founded in Italy in 1899 under the imprint of this movement, through the commitment of Giuseppe Toniolo and the support of the bishop of Padua, Giuseppe Callegari, and the bishop of Pavia, Agostino Riboldi. It was articulated into five sections: the third was dedicated to scientific, natural and mathematical studies and presided over by Maffi, who also directed the new *Rivista di fisica, matematica e scienze naturali* (1900–12), published in Pavia, again with the help of Bishop Riboldi. The magazine was intended primarily for scholastic institutions, seminaries and ecclesiastics. It dealt with many scientific and technical topics, among which photography, optics, geography, biology, zoology, botany, and so on.

Indeed, a love of science and an interest in technical applications enjoyed a certain success in ecclesiastical circles between the nineteenth and twentieth centuries, even in the seminaries of religious orders and congregations. For one, I shall mention the Capuchin Angelo Fiorini of Sassalbo, bishop of Pontremoli since 1899, who invented an electric light switch and an automatic railway hand locking system. All of this also led part of the clergy to take on a positivist mentality: certainly not in the sense of materialism or a naturalistic scientism, but in specific cultural aspects, bound more to the single sciences and their progress.

Among these sciences were ethnology and anthropology, which certainly enjoyed a great success in Italy at the end of the nineteenth century, and, what is more, were marked by a clearly positivist matrix. In 1871, Paolo Mantegazza had founded in Florence the *Archivio per l'Antropologia e l'Etnologia*; in 1880, the aforementioned *Archivio di Psichiatria* of Cesare Lombroso appeared; and in 1893, in Rome, Giuseppe Sergi's magazine, *Archivio di Antropologia*. These new 'sciences of mankind', just as they had been successful in the geographical and colonial field, also exerted a certain influence among the clergy, in particular, among the missionaries.[18]

On the other hand, it was in this particular period that the ethno-anthropological researches discovered photography. 'Photography as chronicle'[19] had already been in use for some time. Then 'travel photography'[20] began, which was used for commercial purposes; however, in order to satisfy the European bourgeois[21] wish for exoticism, it was primarily devoted to the Orient (one need only remember the names of Antonio and Felice Beato, Venetians by birth, but naturalised Englishmen[22]). It was from these experiences that photo-journalism and picture magazines[23] developed at the end of the nineteenth century, as well as an awareness for the documentary potentialities of the photographic means; in 1889 the *British Journal of Photography* foresaw the creation of a great photographic archive 'containing the most complete testimony possible… of the current state of the world' in the conviction that such photographs 'would be useful and precious documents within a century'.[24] Because of its documentary value, photography drew the attention not only of geography but also of anthropology: in particular, the aforementioned Paolo Manegazza,[25] who was—as is well known—the first to hold a chair of Anthropology in an Italian university (in Florence in 1869), was also the first president of the Italian Society of Photography, founded in Florence in 1889.[26] This brought as much to the anthropometric portrait[27] as it did to ethnographic photography.

On the other hand, during the same period, the Società Geografica Italiana, the Società d'Esplorazione Commerciale in Africa and the Società Africana d'Italia were amassing a great deal of photographic material and creating important collections of photographs,[28] prevalently from Africa, with the intent of documenting geography and anthropology.[29] There was a deep ethnographic sensitivity,[30] but the 'pictures of others'[31] would gradually turn into that 'colonial view'[32] that would then augment the use of photography on the part of Italian colonialism.[33] Indeed, while until the 1880s attention was principally set on supplying documents in order to know about *others*, the aim later became one of documenting the colonial undertaking and its 'civilising' action in order to construct and enforce a consensus for colonialism itself.[34] Undoubtedly, these cultural processes also influenced the missionary world: thus the missionary photography that first developed was of an ethno-documentary nature, but it slowly took on the aim of documenting and propagandising the life and evangelising activity of the missionaries.[35] Of course, the missionary view also had a scientific and ethnographic content, however, without evolutionist or positivist implications; indeed, its vision was a unitary and Christian universalistic one. It was not the colonialist view of dominion, even if it was in many ways asymmetric:[36] the photograph was, in any case, a technological sanction of what was perceived as a civilising and redeeming superiority. But added to this was a *pietas* for the rich humanity of those weaker cultures. This, therefore, was the intellectual and spiritual environment in which Leone Nani was formed, one in which he developed a remarkable ability to photograph that he used as a technical means for completing his missionary reports with precise descriptions. And thus he left to posterity an extraordinary repertoire of images of China from the beginning of the twentieth century.

1 Cf. G. Verucci, *L'Italia laica prima e dopo l'U-nità 1848-1876. Anticlericalismo, libero pensiero e ateismo nella società italiana*. Rome-Bari: Laterza, 1981.

2 Leo XIII, *Sancta Dei civitas. Le Opere della Propagazione della fede, della Santa Infanzia di Gesù Cristo e delle Scuole d'Oriente*, in Pontificie Opere Missionarie, Direzione Nazionale Italiana (edited by), *Enchiridion della Chiesa Missionaria*. Bologna: Dehoniane, 1997, p. 123.

3 Cf. L. Wei Tsing Sing, *Le Saint Siège, La France et la Chine sous le pontificat de Léon XIII. Le project de l'établissement d'une nonciature à Pékin et l'affaire du Pei-t'ang*, foreword by R. Saubert. Switzerland, 1966; A. Sohier, 'La nonciature pour Pékin en 1886', in *Nouvelle revue de sciences missionaries*, 24 (1968), pp. 3 ff. For further developments cf. A. Giovagnoli (edited by), *Roma e Pechino. La svolta extraeuropea di Benedetto XV*. Rome: Studium, 1999.

4 A. Spicciani, 'Il cardinale Pietro Maffi, scienziato e organizzatore di cultura', in *Il cardinale Pietro Maffi arcivescovo di Pisa. Primi contributi di ricerca*. Pisa: Pacini, 1983, pp. 33–34.

5 Cf. W. Schivelbusch, *Licht, Schein und Wahn: Auftritte der elektrischen Beleuchtung im 20. Jahrhundert*. Berlin: Ernst & Sohn, 1992.

6 Some considerations in F. De Giorgi, 'Note sulla modernizzazione ecclesiale', in *Rivista di storia contemporanea*, no. 1–2 (1994–95), pp. 194–208.

7 Cf. S. Lanaro, *Nazione e lavoro Saggio sulla cultura borghese in Italia 1870-1925*. Venice: Marsilio, 1979.

8 Cf. W. Settimelli, *La fotografia italiana*, in J.-A. Keim (edited by), *Breve storia della fotografia*. Turin: Einaudi, 1976, p. 116.

9 Cf. *1899. Annuario Ecclesiastico*. Rome: Miliani e Filosini, 1899, pp. 5–6.

10 Cf. P. Eymieu, *La part des croyants dans le progress scientifique au XIXé siècle*, 2 vols. Paris, 1920, repr. 1932.

11 Cf. *Congrès scientifique international des catholiques tenue à Paris due 8 au 13 avril 1888*, 2 vols. Paris: Bureaux des 'Annales de Philosophie Chrétienne', 1889; R. de Scoraille, 'Deux Congrès des Savants catholiques', in *Etudes*, 26 (1888), pl. 44, pp. 94–109.

12 Cf. G. Giovannozzi, 'Il terzo Congresso degli scienziati cattolici a Bruxelles', in *La Rassegna Nazionale*, 80 (1894), pp. 545–66 and 81 (1895), pp. 518–22.

13 Cf. G. Giovannozzi, 'Il quarto Congresso internazionale degli scienziati cattolici', in *La Rassegna Nazionale*, 98 (1897), pp. 5–26.

14 Cf. A. Ratti, 'Ricordi e riflessioni di un italiano sul IV Congresso internazionale scientifico dei cattolici a Friburgo', in *Rivista internazionale di scienze sociali e discipline ausiliarie*, 5 (1897), pp. 490–97.

15 Cf. G. Faraoni, 'Un Congresso scientifico', in *Studi religiosi* (1901), pp. 53–75.

16 Cf. A.Baudrillart, *Vie de Mgr d'Hulst*, vol. 1. Paris, 1921, pp. 545–61.

17 Cf. A. Michieli, 'Albert de Lapparent', in *Rivista di fisica, matematica e scienze naturali*, 9 (1908), pp. 225–42.

18 Cf. S. Puccini, 'Evoluzionismo e positivismo nell'antropologia italiana (1896-1911)', in *L'antropologia italiana. Un secolo di storia*. Rome-Bari: Laterza, 1985, pp. 97–148; A. R. Leone, 'La Chiesa, I cattolici e le scienze dell'uomo: 1860-1960', *ibid.*, pp. 51–96.

19 Cf. I. Zannier, *Storia e tecnica della fotografia*. Rome-Bari: Laterza, 2001[7], p. 149.

20 *Ibid.*, p. 150.

21 Cf. Ch.-H. Favrod (edited by), *Etranges Étrangers. Photographie et exotisme. 1850-1910*. Paris: Centre National de la Photographie, 1989; B. Cappelli and E. Cocco (edited by), *Esotismo e crisi della civiltà*. Naples, Tempi moderni, 1979; G. Freund, *Fotografia e società*. Turin: Einaudi, 1974, pp. 48–83.

22 Antonio and Felice Beato worked in the Orient: 'they were there for the first time in 1857, after the war experience of the Crimea at the end of 1855 together with their brother-in-law James Robertson, with whom they finished the famous reportage of Fenton; they then undertook a long journey, part of which with Robertson, that took them to photograph in Palestine, India, China, Japan, Sudan, an interminable adventure that lasted almost a lifetime' (Zannier, *Storia e tecnica della fotografia*, p. 151). Also of note is that 'John Thomson (1837–1921), journalist and writer, after having studied a little chemistry, left for Ceylon in 1862, and went as far as Malacca, India and China, where he photographed "street scenes" of exceptional vitality for those times' (*ibid.*, p. 154).

23 Cf. at least F. Surdich, 'Aspetti e immagini delle culture extraeuropee nelle prime riviste illustrate italiane', in *Saggi di storia del giornalismo in memoria di L. Balestrieri*, Quaderni dell'Istituto Mazziniano, 2. Genoa, 1982.

24 Quoted in B. Newhall, *The history of photography : from 1839 to the present*, 5th ed. Boston: Little, Brown, 1988. Cf. also A. Gilardi, *Storia sociale della fotografia*. Milan: Mondadori, 2000.

25 Cf. P. Chiozzi, 'Fotografia e antropologia nell'opera di Paolo Mantegazza (1831-1910)', in *Archivio Fotografico Toscano*, 6 (1987), pp. 56–61.

26 Cf. L. Tomassini, 'Le origini della Società Fotografica Italiana e lo sviluppo della fotografia in Italia. Appunti e problemi', in *Archivio Fotografico Toscano*, I (1985); C. Panerai, 'Fotografia e antropologia nel "Bollettino della Società Fotografica Italiana". Una promessa disattesa', in *Archivio Fotografico Toscano*, 13 (1991).

27 Cf. A. Baldi, 'Uso e valenze del ritratto fotografico nelle scienze antropologiche', in *Archivio Fotografico Toscano*, 3 (1986); E. Prando, 'Note sui rapporti tra fotografia e antropologia', in *Rivista di storia e critica della fotografia*, 3 (1981), pp. 61–65.

28 Cf. M. Mancini (edited by), *Obiettivo sul mondo. Viaggi ed esplorazioni nelle immagini dell'Archivio Fotografico della Società Geografica Italiana (1866-1956)*. Rome: Società Geografica Italiana, 1996; A. Triulzi, 'Napoli e l'immagine dell'Africa nella collezione fotografica della Società Africana d'Italia (circa 1880-1940)', in E. Casti and A. Turco (edited by), *Culture dell'alterità. Il territorio africano e le sue rappresentazioni*. [Milan]: Unicopli, 1999, pp. 185–205; S. Palma, 'La fototeca dell'istituto Italo Africano', in *Africa* (1989), pp. 605–6; S. Palma, 'Raccolte fotografiche', in A. Triulzi (edited by), *L'Africa dall'immaginario alle immagini. Scritti e immagini dell'Africa nei fondi della Biblioteca Reale*. Turin: Il Salone del Libro, 1989.

29 *Etnie. La scuola antropologica fiorentina e la fotografia tra '800 e '900*. Florence: Fratelli Alinari, 1996.

30 Cf. A. Baldi, 'L'impiego della fotografia nell'indagine di carattere etnoantropologico all'interno del periodo coloniale italiano', in *Rivista di storia e critica della fotografia*, 4, 5 (1983), pp. 23–53.

31 Cf. S. Palma, 'L'alterità in posa. La rappresentazione dell'Africa nella prima fotografia coloniale italiana', in C. Cerretti (edited by), *Colonie africane e cultura italiana fra Ottocento e Novecento. Le esplorazioni e la geografia*. Rome: CISU, 1995, pp. 75–86.

32 Cf. N. Labanca, 'Uno sguardo coloniale. Immagine e propaganda nelle fotografie e nelle illustrazioni del primo colonialismo italiano (1882-1896)', in *Archivio Fotografico Toscano*, 8 (1988), pp. 43–61.

33 Cf. L. Goglia, *Colonialismo e fotografia. Il caso italiano 1885-1940*. Messina: Sicania, 1989; *Fotografie e colonialismo, I*, special issue of the *Rivista di storia e critica della fotografia* (1981). Cf. also G. Campassi and M. T. Sega, 'Uomo bianco, donna nera. L'immagine della donna nella fotografia coloniale', in *Rivista di storia e critica della fotografia*, 4, 5 (1983), pp. 54–62.

34 Cf. A. Triulzi, 'Fotografia coloniale e storia dell'Africa', in *Archivio Fotografico Toscano*, 8 (1988), pp. 34–37.

35 Cf. S. Rivoir, 'Per la propagazione della fede. Appunti per una storia delle fotografie delle missioni cattoliche', in *Fotografie e colonialismo*.

36 Cf., in general the acute observations of C. Ginzburg, *Rapporti di forza. Storia, retorica, prova*. Milan: Feltrinelli, 2000; and E. W. Said, *Culture and Imperialism*, 1st ed. New York: Knopf, 1993.

China at the Beginning of the Twentieth Century

Sergio Ticozzi

Father Leone Nani left Italy in September 1903 and on 22 January of the following year he arrived in China at Guluba, in the centre of what was then the Apostolic Vicariate of southern Shaanxi; he would remain there until the summer of 1914. The Vicariate then included the two civic prefectures of Hanzhong, the capital, and Xing'an for a total of 28 large villages and about five million inhabitants.

'As for the climate—wrote Father Nani—this is a place that is perennially damp, since rice paddies cover the vast plains and also because of the periodic annual rains. The wealth of the land comes for the most part from different rivers, whose waters are essential for the maintenance of the rice paddies; and its river, the Han, which rises in this area, not only provides large catches of fish, but also favours and still ensures commercial traffic as far as Hankou. The population, in addition to occupying itself with the cultivation of rice, which is daily bread for the Chinese, also keeps busy in small trade and much of the local production is also exported from the province.'[1]

Father Nani, driven by the fervour of his missionary vocation and an exuberant enthusiasm as well as by a youthful spirit of adventure (he had just turned 23), was anxious to reach his mission. But what kind of social and political world was he about to venture into?

The Chinese Empire, then in a period of radical transition, was engaged in remedying the inefficiency of the Manchu Qing court, dominated since 1898 by the Dowager Empress Cixi (1835–1908). The transition had come about because of the need to modernise the country's structures and institutions. The diffusion of new ideas, however, was accompanied by discontent, abuses and disorders, which had been on the increase for some time and resulted in diverse revolutionary demonstrations and revolts. Bandits and criminals, who roamed round the countryside in well-organised bands, took advantage of the confusion to oppress the population.

Furthermore, the relations with foreign powers had become tense; the latter's actions and demands could no longer be disregarded. The aggressive policy towards China, especially on the part of France, England, Holland, Belgium, Russia, the United States, Italy and Japan, had become increasingly bolder. Their objective was clear: to split up the Empire into different spheres of influence. In order to justify itself in some way and calm popular discontent, the Qing court tried to put the blame for its own decline and disorders on foreign arrogance; to this end it gave its support to the movement of the Boxers—the 'Righteous and Harmonious Fists' (*Yihequan*).[2] In the spring of 1900, in fact, with official court backing, the Boxers launched a violent uprising against all foreigners, including the Christian missionaries and even the converted Chinese. For the majority of the people it was not easy to distinguish between political and religious operators, given the close ties and cooperation existing between them. The attacks spread rapidly, above all throughout northern China. Some thirty thousand Chinese Christians were killed, among whom seven priests and five seminarians in addition to five bishops, seven foreign nuns and thirty-nine missionaries. Among these was Father Alberico Crescitelli, a fellow brother of Father Nani, who was martyred with other Chinese neophytes at Yanzibian, at the mission Nani was bound for (21 July 1900).[3]

In the meantime, the continuous attacks against their legations and the murders of diplomatic personnel brought about the intervention of eight foreign powers, especially after the promulgation of an official order to expel all foreigners and eliminate the Christians. A combined European military force of about two thousand soldiers was dispatched from Tianjin in order to go to the aid of the foreign legations of Peking, which were liberated in the middle of August 1900. After various treaties, a protocol was signed: the foreign powers again asked China to disarm, to pay a massive indemnity and to accept other heavy conditions (7 September 1901). One of the consequences was the beginning of the 'Italian concession' at Tianjin.[4]

The brutal conduct of the Boxers cast a bad light on China in the eyes of the world, while the demonstration of foreign arrogance instead favoured the spread of xenophobic feelings among the Chinese population. Another significant consequence of the Boxer uprising was the total humiliation of the imperial government. This, combined with the foreigners' sense of supremacy and their extremely tough behaviour, forced the official circles to change their attitude towards the Westerners, who now became the object of a mixture of hostility, respect and fear.

The new ideas meanwhile spread rapidly and even in Shaanxi there emerged a need for modernisation. The centre of diffusion of this new ferment was the schools. Intellectuals returning from universities, also from foreign ones, became part of the teaching corps and began to stimulate the minds of the young. The new generation's eagerness to learn the 'new knowledge', that is, 'popular' culture with modern values, and its subsequent rejection of tradition, considered stagnant and oppressive, facilitated the weakening of resistance against the West. But it also augmented popular discontent and disorder.

The revolutionary ferment against the Empire became more and more acute, above all in central and southern China, under the guidance of Sun Yat-sen (1866–1925). The latter, with his new United League for China, founded in August 1905, organised various revolts (six of remarkable scale between 1906 and 1911), which inflicted a tremendous blow on the Qing court.

The situation in the Vicariate of Shaanxi remained in ebullition until 1908. One reads in the *Missioni cattoliche* (Catholic Missions): 'There is an insistent rumour that a great anti-dynastic revolution will soon break out. I do not know how much truth there is to this, but the fact remains that by now the whole system is based on colossal thievery: the great Mandarins are thieves as are the lesser ones. Oppression has reached the limit and Peking, which has taken no steps, is considered responsible for everything… The people are tired, the students who return from Japan, America and Europe, in the hope of fishing in troubled waters, are blowing on the fire… Certainly, innovation is necessary, but not much good can be hoped for from a revolution of fire'.[5]

The different uprisings resulted in the revolt of Wuchang on 10 October 1911, which quickly spread to all the other provinces and led to the fall of the Empire when the boy emperor Xuantong was on the throne (Puyi, 1905–1967, ruled 1909–11).

But with the declaration of the Republic at the beginning of 1912 and its first halting steps, problems were basically left unresolved. The political and social situation remained muddled and, because of the widespread presence of bandit and criminal bands, it continued to worsen. The young Chinese Republic could barely hold itself up. The lack of union among its leaders, especially those at the top, was manifested by counter-revolutionary attempts. The atmosphere was one of total anarchy, punctuated by frequent uprisings. In Hanzhong, immediately after the end of the celebrations for the first anniversary of the Republic, the soldiers, who had not been paid for some time, began to rebel and loot, terrorising the population. The city depopulated in no time at all, its inhabitants fleeing to the mountains, in particular, the women who feared the ferocity of the soldiers. The rebels, who were soon joined by bandits and adventurers, sacked the banks and wealthier residences above all. Meanwhile, however, the new ideas continued to spread and take root, and distrust in the traditional culture and beliefs increased leading to the Movement of 4 May 1919 and the proclamation of the 'new culture' and the modern values of science and democracy.

The religious context

'There is almost total ruin', reported the bishop of Peking, Monsignor Alfonso Favier (1837–1905) after the Boxer tragedy. 'Forty years of hard work have been wiped out, but not the courage of the missionaries, who are sure of a good result because "the blood of martyrs is the seed of Christians".'[6] Indeed, after this storm the situation of the Catholic Church in China proved to be more propitious. The defeat and the shame suffered also forced the Qing court to change its attitude towards the missionaries and foreign churches. As a result, in 1902, the Dowager Empress conceded an audience to the bishop of Peking himself. In the *Memorial of two members of the Chinese Ministry of Public Instruction* of 1905,[7] the official treatment reserved to foreigners and missionaries was specified: 'We must show ourselves to be kind towards them, since this is ordered by the Treaties. We must let them preach freely, since we cannot prevent it. On the other hand, however, they must not interfere in the affairs of others. Further, we must not forget that they are our guests, and if treated as such, they will have a good opinion of us and will in turn treat us kindly. We must not oppress them, only fear them a little and, above all, show no contempt. We must simply adhere to the conditions fixed by the Treaties and the rules of friendship. In past times, we have repeatedly treated the Europeans badly: this was unjust and we acted, in those cases, exactly like someone who receives a person of consequence in his home without offering him tea. This behaviour must be changed'.

A period of transition then followed that was quite favourable for Christian evangelisation. The historian of Christian missions, Kenneth Scott Latourette describes it in entirely positive terms: 'With the suppression of the Boxer rebellion, a new era in the history of China began and with it a new chapter in the history of the Church…. In general, especially in the first two decades of 1900, the missionaries had free rein. Never before in the history of the Church had there been so great a number of non-Christians so accessible mentally and physically to the Gospels…. The time of greatest opportunity was from the end of 1901 to the outbreak of the First World War'.[8]

According to the statistics, the number of Catholics rose from 720,540 in 1900 to 888,131 in 1906 and to 1,432,000 in 1912. The number of missionaries also increased: above all, the French, Italian and German ones. The Jesuits in particular were engaged mainly in scientific-literary educational activities, opening, among other things, Aurora University in Shanghai in 1903. In practice, however, the missionaries still continued be the object both of flattery, thereby enjoying privileges and protection, and of antagonism and hostility on the part of many people and the Chinese authorities in general. In 1908, moreover, in order to eliminate a certain climate of discontent, the 'official rank' of foreign missionaries, which had been conceded in 1899, was abolished by the Chinese government. The missionaries took advantage of the more favourable conditions to occupy themselves more diligently in their work of 'converting the pagans' in line with their previous methods. Their apostolate consisted in travelling from one Christian community to the other using whatever transport was at hand, and in sending catechists there. Besides the administration of the sacraments and catechesis, they also carried out works of charity, instruction and social assistance. This is the testimony of a Chinese priest in 1913: 'Among the pagans the most advantageous works are schools, orphanages and dispensaries. The dispensaries are very useful, not for the selling of medicines, but for healing with a charitable spirit the corporal and spiritual maladies of the people… The orphanages among the pagans are indispensable for saving many souls, because everyone knows that the Chinese have a terrible custom of abandoning baby girls, who, however, are brought to the orphanage…. The schools, then, are really necessary here for teaching the Christian doctrine and prayers to the sons and daughters of the new Christians…'.[9]

Although methods and mentality continued in the wake of tradition, the signs and premonitions of innovation began to be perceived. The period following the Republican Revolution and the war therefore turned out to be a difficult one for the Church in China, but also one of a certain significance thanks to new impulses that pushed it in the direction of a real maturity. Unfortunately, the challenge of renewal was perceived only by a limited number of people, while the great majority still followed the ancient methods without any substantial changes.

The initiatives of the Chinese Catholics were significant in opposing the declaration of Confucianism as the state religion and in making sure that the freedom of religion was included in the national Constitution of 1914.

The efforts of the Holy See also continued to meliorate the apostolic undertakings and methods. However, one of the major obstacles that still remained was the colonial powers' right to protect Catholic missions. The Portuguese *padroado* had been greatly reduced, but the French protectorate, envied and claimed by the governments of other countries, in particular, Germany and Italy, continued to dominate. The Holy See had been attempting to establish direct relations with the Chinese government since the 1880s in an effort to resolve the situation, but the hostile attitude of the French government had caused every attempt to fail.

When, in 1904, the separation between the State and the Church was established in France and diplomatic relations broken off with the Holy See, Rome again tried, as it did also in 1914, to set up direct relations with China, but without any substantial results. Other European powers, including Italy, continued, moreover, to intrigue in order to impose their protection on their own missions.

Another attempt was made in 1917 by the former Chinese foreign minister Lu Zheng Xiang,[10] and then again in the spring of 1918, but once again unsuccessfully, because the French complained that their protectorate rights had been violated. In a short time the issue involved most of the Chinese Christian communities. The Holy See tried to persuade the French episcopate of the virtue of its initiative and to urge its support, but in vain. It was necessary to wait until 1922 and the mission of the Apostolic Delegation in China for the problem to be finally resolved.

The situation of the Vicariate of southern Shaanxi

The former bishop of the Vicariate of Shaanxi, Monsignor Pio Giuseppe Passerini (1866–1918), wrote in February 1901: 'Since that time [that is, since the martyrdom of St Alberico, *editor's note*], in spite of the still disquieting threats, the state of things has improved and, in conclusion, we were forced to interrupt our ministry only for three months. But while our bereavements, thank God, have been less than those of other missions, our material losses have, in any case, been enormous…'.[11]

In the following years, the movement of conversions proved to be promising: 'Although it has not yet occurred in other provinces, peace and quiet in this Vicariate have been confirmed more and more and one can really say that the Church is presently enjoying great favour, not only among the people, but also with the civil and military authorities. The current prestige of the Church is still a reason for some to become Christian; therefore we are very careful and quite cautious in accepting new converts, choosing to examine them well first…'.[12]

At the beginning of 1904, there were slightly over 11,000 Catholics and 1850 catechumens (out of about five million inhabitants) in the Vicariate in some forty churches and chapels; there were seventeen Italian missionaries and four Chinese priests, and also present was a group of Canossian nuns who ran an orphanage, a clinic and a school at Guluba. In the following years, the news continued to be quite positive. But in 1908, when the circumstances became more alarming, the bishop called all the foreign missions back to the two principal cities, Guluba and Hanzhong, leaving the Chinese priests to work in the districts.

In 1910, in Hanzhong itself, the construction of a cathedral was underway, but the political situation was worsening. In November 1911, the bishop informed: '…up to now, notwithstanding the outbreak of an anti-dynastic revolution in this province, we are moving ahead without any ominous incidents…. They say that in Xi'an, the capital of all of Shaanxi, there has been a real massacre in the quarter of the Mancasi…. At Hanzhong, the mission's headquarters, the Mandarins are protecting us as they should, and, considering that the church is a safe place, some of them have entrusted us with their most important documents; some bankers have done the same and have even begged us to shelter those dearest to them in some of our houses…. Owing to the general panic in the city, there is a stampede of pagans and Christians in the countryside, especially in some places…'.[13].

As the danger drew closer, even the missionaries prepared to defend themselves with the means and personnel on hand: at Hanzhong there were four fathers with about fifty Christians and at Guluba approximately one hundred people with all the other missionaries. Referring to the armed defence in the Catholic quarters, Father Nani wrote: 'But this precaution was to prepare some sort of defence in advance; or at least the appearance of a defence that had a truly providential and magical effect. Some zinc pipes could easily be taken for cannons, with tins of Dutch cheese serving as shells. These were placed in the windows of the Residence (which was in the Town), while Monsignor's crosier, broken in two, was stationed at the front door pointing at the street to give the impression of two lethal mouths of firearms…'.[14]

The first to rebel against the imperial forces and join the Republican Revolution was the prefecture of Xing'an. This incurred fear among the imperial authorities in Hanzhong, who were threatened by the approaching revolutionaries, who would soon reach Xixiang, a two-day march away. The imperial troops sent there succeeded in defeating the revolutionaries and reconquering Xixiang. But it was a temporary victory, because violent clashes between the two parties and between other military groups resumed very quickly, and Hanzhong passed under the control of the revolutionary forces. At the beginning of 1912, the mission also passed under the control of the new Chinese Republic. Together with the alarming information about the attacks on Hanzhong and Guluba, false news also circulated about the destruction of the Vicariate and the murder of the Vicar and other missionaries, which the Italian minister himself reported. The local missionaries were not particularly impressed, occupied as they were in trying to stay clear of both the old and the new local authorities in a rather delicate situation. The imperial officials, in fact, after having been forced to leave their positions, had asked and obtained shelter in the residences of the Catholic Church.

'The new officials' Father Nani informed, 'had to yield the royal power to a thousand self-styled soldiers, armed to the teeth, coming from Sichuan, who were trying to grab all the available silver and money. Considering that there was not much, it was necessary to convoke an assembly and discuss the matter better with all the parties involved, including the local disarmed ones. Among the more important orders of the day was the insidious decision that the ex authorities, now guests of the Church, should return to the town for further negotiations. This was clearly a pretext for stripping them of all they had and slaughtering them. To expedite this, embassies were sent to the Church, ordering them to hand over their sought-after guests. The latter of course knew full well that once they were outside, they would fall into the hands of executioners, and naturally they energetically refused to obey such an absurd order. In the thorny controversy that ensued in several days of excited discussion, the Church held firm to its rights, and especially to its duty of charitable love. Finally they succeeded in refusing to comply with the lawless intentions of these arrogant intruders and kept their guests in safety. The townsfolk who were witnesses of these negotiations loudly applauded this shining act of charity'.[15]

The matter was finally resolved with the control of the Republican troops of Xi'an. As soon as the Hanzhong authorities who were guests of the Catholic mission were sure of their salvation, they returned safe and sound to their families, after having expressed their gratitude to the mission. Once peace returned, the building of the new cathedral and other works began again in Hanzhong, and the missionaries returned to their apostolate and visits. There was one critical moment during the disorders, which has already been mentioned, on the occasion of the first anniversary of the Republic. The church, by then almost finished, was spared, but the bishop had to interrupt the building works when the Church lost a sum of money, albeit not great, after the banks had been looted.

Once the storm had passed, the construction of the new cathedral and other works resumed. The bells arrived from Italy, and at the beginning of December it was possible to solemnly bless the church and at the same time celebrate Monsignor Passerini's fiftieth anniversary as a priest. The official photographer for the occasion was none other than Father Nani.

Father Nani not only took the photos, but he also furnished a description of the celebration, at which there were 'imposing and ritualistic religious services that made the Christians proud, edified the catechumens, and astonished so many poor pagans… [services] which would add a glorious new page to the lustre and growth of his Vicariate; indeed, they so astounded the entire pagan population that, as if bewitched simply by exposure to the feasts celebrated, they arrived not only from the crowded surroundings but also from distant villages and cities, pouring through the gates of the biggest city, Hanzhong, in such numbers that the streets overflowed with all kinds of people, all of whom headed uninterruptedly towards the Catholic residence…. Never before, everyone said, had such a boisterous and incalculable throng of people been seen, as in this circumstance; and it continued for a good four days from dawn to dusk until the last flash of fireworks and illuminations…'.[16]

After the celebration, life returned to normal and apostolic commitments resumed with greater zeal. Monsignor Passerini was particularly attentive in supplying the Vicariate with churches and residences: at his death in 1918, sixteen had been built. He was succeeded in 1919 by Monsignor Antonio Maria Capettini (1877–1958), who, until he was forced by illness to return home in 1925, increased his efforts, above all in the educational sector, opening schools and providing them with good teachers, thanks to the foundation in 1922 of the Pia Unione delle Maestre della Dottrina cristiana (Holy Union of Teachers of Christian Doctrine). The seed of Christianity, that was sown those years and contributed to by the missionary zeal of Father Nani, gave and continues to give fruit, as it grows amid many difficulties without ever being beaten down or uprooted.

[1] Quoted in *Un inviato italiano nello Shensi [Shaanxi] meridionale*. Rome, PIME General Archive, Father Leone Nani file.

[2] For a good description of the movement, see Immanuel C. Y. Hasu, *The Rise of Modern China*, 5th ed. New York and Oxford: Oxford University Press, 1995.

[3] One hundred and twenty of these martyrs were canonised on 1 October 2000.

[4] The 'Italian concession' in Tianjin, which measured half of a square kilometre, was ceded with the agreement of 7 June 1902. The Italian presence would end with the armistice of 8 September 1943 when the Japanese occupied it without encountering any resistance. In the Paris Peace Treaty of 1947, which ended the Second World War, Italy renounced all the rights it had previously enjoyed in China.

[5] *Le Missioni Cattoliche*, 1908, p. 136.

[6] *Le Missioni Cattoliche*, 1901, p. 26.

[7] Reported in *Zuo Shun-Sheng, Zhongguo Jinbainian Shizilian Chuobian* (Documents relative to the last hundred years of Chinese history). Shanghai, 1926.

[8] K. Scott Latourette, *A History of Christian Missions in China*. New York: MacMillan Company, 1929, pp. 527, 533–34.

[9] P. Simone Ly, 'Esortazione di un Cinese alla gioventù d'Italia', in *Il Missionario cattolico*, 1913, pp. 54–55.

[10] Lu Zheng Xiang (1871–1949): son of a Protestant minister, he had begun his diplomatic career in the Chinese Empire in 1892, working at the Chinese Embassy in Moscow. With the advent of the Republic, he continued to be active politically, becoming Minister of Foreign Affairs. He converted to the Catholic Church and later became a Benedictine monk at the Abbey of St Andrew in Belgium with the name of Dom Pierre Celestine. He described his inter-cultural religious experience in the work *Le vie di Confucio e di Cristo*.

[11] *Le Missioni Cattoliche*, 1901, p. 73.

[12] Letter of Monsignor P. Passerini, 18 October 1901, published in *Periodico mensile delle Missioni Estere*, 1901, p. 177.

[13] *Il Missionario Cattolico*, X, 1, January–February 1912, p. 9.

[14] Rome, PIME General Archive, Father Leone Nani file.

[15] *Ibid.*

[16] In the issue of *Il Missionario Cattolico* dedicated to the festivity (XI, 12, 20 December 1913, p. 180) one reads: 'The clichés of this issue of the Bulletin and those that we will publish subsequently are reproductions of beautiful and admirable photographs that were sent to us by our missionaries, especially by the talented and clever Don Leone Nani, who was so kind as to prepare a great, varied, and splendid collection for us'.

Province of Shaanxi

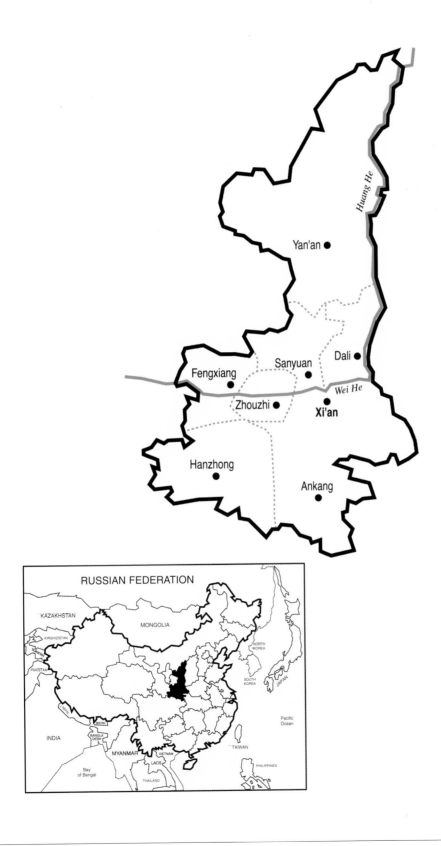

Italy and China: Two Millennia of Encounters

Federico Masini

No other Western country can boast such a long history of relations with China as Italy which, according to Chinese sources, was known to those far lands at least from the time that the Emperor 'Andun', that is Marcus Aurelius Antoninus, sent an embassy in 166 BC to the emperors of the Han dynasty, who had ruled in China for more than three centuries. The Roman Empire inspired so much respect among those ancient Chinese that they called it the Empire of 'Daqin', that is, Great China.

Our ancient Romans also seem to have had an echo of that distant and powerful Asian Empire, which they called 'Seres' (from which the Italian word *serico*, meaning of silk), because the Roman matrons loved that precious fabric so much that Horace thundered against their excessive spending to possess it. We do not have, however, news of any direct contact; no Roman or Chinese traveller has left any trace of a possible journey to such far-off places.[1]

The first travellers to leave written documents about their journeys—destined to bring China closer to Italy during the centuries—reached there when the Mongolian Empire, then extending over all of Asia, had consented to the arrival of Italian merchants and travellers. The most famous—although not the only one—was Marco Polo, whose travel diary made it possible for the known world to expand and to embrace Asia and even the Americas. When Christopher Columbus embarked in Genoa, he carried a copy of *Il Milione* with him, the only testimony then available regarding the distance of those Oriental lands in the West that he was seeking to reach by sea.

In addition to merchants, the *pax mongolica* enabled Christian missionaries to go to China, for the most part Franciscans, who, by land and at the cost of enormous sacrifices and extreme dangers, tried to reach the court of the Mongol emperors who were ruling at Peking with the idea of making alliances and even converting the leaders of those armies that inspired such fear in the Europe of the first decades of the thirteenth century. Those travellers failed in their missionary objective, but thanks to their descriptions of the habits, customs and beliefs of the Mongols and Chinese, they made it possible for Europe to begin to know those faraway people better.[2] As missionaries and men of the Church, they were, in fact, accustomed to writing reports and drawing up documents; their reports therefore proved to be much more precise and detailed than Marco Polo's *Milione*. In any case, perhaps because they were in Latin, or perhaps because they did not contain marvellous and amazing facts that then like now attract a reading public, they never managed to rival the fame of the book that Marco Polo dictated in 1298 in the Genoese prisons which has instead enjoyed such an extraordinary success.[3]

As for all these travellers, merchants and Italian religious, there seems to be no trace of them in Chinese historical works, which are, however, rich in information and data about the populations that sent embassies to the imperial court. The only exception is the mention, in the history of the Mongol dynasty (Yuanshi), of a gift brought to Peking by Giovanni de' Marignolli in 1342: a marvellous Neapolitan horse. The Chinese do not seem to have appreciated or considered worthy of note in their historical works anything else from the West, neither man nor object.

Several centuries had to pass before some trace of Italy appeared in Chinese works, to the time when a new 'team' of missionaries, who were also endowed with great physical and intellectual ability, took on the enormous task of converting the Peking court.[4] Towards the end of the sixteenth century, when the great geographical discoveries opened the sea routes to the Indies, Portuguese and Italian Jesuits settled in Macao on the southern shores of the Chinese Empire—then governed by the autochthonal Ming dynasty—and from there began their cultural advance into China. In just a few years, many of them succeeded in making themselves appreciated at the court of Peking for the cultural gifts and scientific knowledge they had accumulated during hard years of study at the Collegio Romano, one of the finest universities of the time. They were Italians for the most part: Michele Ruggieri, who arrived in China in 1581 and could boast the merit of having paved the way for his fellow brothers; Matteo Ricci, the founder of the missions who, by bringing Western culture and science, in particular geography and geometry, to China, was the first to elaborate the missionary method that brought so much success to the Jesuits in that country;[5] Giulio Alemi, who composed extraordinary geographical works of scientific and cultural divulgation in Chinese, primary sources for the study of the West on the part of Chinese men of letters until the end of the nineteenth century;[6] Martino Martini, whose main interest was to inform Europe about Chinese geography and history, and who wrote works in Latin that were incomparable fonts of knowledge about China for Westerners (an atlas of his, dated 1655, is conserved in the Museo Popoli e Culture del PIME in Milan);[7] Filippo Grimaldi, who thanks to his correspondence with European scientists like Gottfried W. Leibniz contributed to the diffusion of Chinese scientific knowledge in the West and brought modern technological inventions in turn to China. Many other Jesuit missionaries made Italy and Europe and science and Christianity known to Chinese scholars, while bringing news about Chinese philosophy, history and geography to Europe.[8] It was an extraordinary season of knowledge, reciprocal in part and intense as it was brief: in fact, it brusquely came to an end early in the eighteenth century when the Jesuits in China were accused by the missionaries of other orders of having exaggerated in their desire to understand and accept China and its civil rites honouring the wise Confucius, rites that in their eyes were pagan acts.[9]

When this season of exchanges came to an end, Italy's guiding role in the relations between the Western world and China progressively diminished: the supremacy of the seas passed from the hands of the Catholic crowns of Spain and Portugal to those of Protestant England, and the cultural centre of Europe moved inexorably north towards France and, above all, to England. China was no longer simply a land of missionary conquest, but a continent of economic and commercial conquest, a place to buy goods to export to the West, porcelain and tea primarily, and to sell goods that were not otherwise marketable, in particular opium: a business maintained by gunboats and armies, which were always ready to intervene whenever economic interests were undermined or simply jeopardized.[10]

Thus, Italy disappeared from the front line, but it continued to make an incisive contribution when the English crown's commercial and military campaigns began, by providing the cultural and linguistic mediation of Chinese interpreters, who had trained in Naples at the Collegio de' Cinesi that Matteo Ripa had established in 1732, and who took part in the first English missions to the imperial court as interpreters of Latin and Chinese.[11]

After the Italian Franciscan and Jesuit missionaries had been employed for centuries in spreading knowledge of the West in China, in the nineteenth century, English, German and later American Protestant missionaries took over the task of diffusing Western culture in that country, a culture and a science that was quite different from the one the Italians had attempted to introduce in the previous centuries. Thus, Italy, which had been celebrated in the works published in Chinese by the Jesuits in the seventeenth century as the cradle of an ancient civilisation, the

home of the modern sciences of geography and astronomy and the centre of all Christianity became a borderland country, famed for its internal divisions, populated by bandits and governed by corrupt aristocrats and a totally decadent Church[12] in the works written in Chinese by Protestant missionaries.

Indeed, in the first decades of the nineteenth century, by adopting a strategy that was opposite to that of their predecessors, the Protestant missionaries dedicated themselves to the conversion of the lower classes of the population, and only later on became interested in the proselytism of the upper classes of Chinese society. Missionary work was considered to be consistent with the development of commercial, economic and political relations with the moribund Chinese Empire. The local ruling class seemed incapable of responding to this concentric fire of belligerent, political, cultural and scientific pressures: the Protestant missionaries in fact printed scientific journals and founded cultural associations, their governments forced China to establish diplomatic relations, under the control of the war arsenals of the Western powers, who were always ready to intervene at the slightest tremor of the Chinese government. Italy appears to have been absent from Chinese history during the first half of the nineteenth century. The few Italians active in China those years were working for other Western countries: Giuseppe Calleri, a resident of Paris, reached China first as a missionary and then as a diplomat with the French consulate in Canton;[13] Giuseppe Garibaldi, according to some English witnesses, cruised the Canton sea as the commander of a merchant ship; or more simply, the many sailors who embarked on Western ships in action in Chinese waters.[14]

The Italian missionaries were also able to operate during those years, but only under the 'safety cover' of a European nation: in fact, during the entire nineteenth century, France was able to boast the complete patronage of all missionaries, religious orders and Catholic congregations throughout China, both Chinese and foreign.

The situation began to change in 1866, when the Kingdom of Italy finally decided to send its first diplomatic mission to the Far East with the aim of stipulating trade negotiations with China and Japan, which were finally completed amidst a thousand difficulties and reciprocal misunderstandings.[15]

In any case, France also opposed an agreement reached between the Holy See and China in 1886 regarding the reciprocal establishment of diplomatic legations, so that the Holy See was unable to eliminate the French control of missionary activity in that country.[16] The conditions of Catholic missions in China during the entire nineteenth century were extremely precarious; they were controlled by France and crushed by the pressure exercised by the North European powers who supported their Protestant missionaries with the force of arms, trade levies and financial assistance for important cultural and scientific activities. All this was going on in a country then on the brink of economic, political and social collapse, brought about by sanguinary peasant revolts (such as that of the Taiping in which blood was shed in central and southern China for several years); a country governed by a ruling class torn between trying to resist the excessive power of the Western troops with arms and the attempts of passive resistance pursued by the imperial court and the Mandarin class in the name of ethical-moral principles that were absolutely unsuitable for opposing the pressing, yet violent modernity.

The old century came to an end with the bloody Boxer rebellion, an extreme attempt to oppose the Christian West on the part of the Chinese popular masses whose protest was quickly supported by the imperial court.

This was the China in which Father Leone Nani promised, in Rome in 1900, to conduct his missionary activity; he arrived there shortly thereafter by ship, disembarking at Shanghai, and then continuing along the Yangtze river to Hankou, whence he reached his final destination, the mission of Hanzhong in the province of Shaanxi. Although it was an inaccessible and remote place in central-eastern China, it could, however, boast an extraordinary missionary tradition from the time a stone stele of 781 was found near Xi'an in 1625, bearing witness to the diffusion of Nestorian Christianity in China (a cast of the stele is exhibited in the Museo Popoli e Culture del PIME in Milan). The discovery of the stele had sparked an extraordinary interest in those places, and, as a consequence, missionaries had been present there almost uninterruptedly since the first half of the seventeenth century.[17] Father Nani carried out his own apostolate for about a decade, and so witnessed the end of the Chinese Empire (10 October 1911) and the foundation of the Republic (11 January 1912), albeit as a peripheral observer with respect to the political and military events that were going on during those turbulent years. He did not succeed, however, in being present when Benedict XV ascended to the papal throne, nor did he hear about the repercussions in Holy See politics when the Pope announced his intention to establish direct relations with the new Chinese government. In fact, Nani returned to Italy in 1914 for reasons of health, bringing with him a rich store of information about China, one that was not about to be printed in Latin for erudite Westerners, but printed instead from photographic plates. This new means would be an aid for those who really wished to learn about China and understand it, rather than simply judge it.

[1] For the history of the relations between Italy and China, see in particular G. Bertuccioli and F. Masini, *Italia e Cina*. Bari: Laterza, 1996 [Chinese translation: *Yidali yu Zhongguo*. Beijing: Shangwu yinshuguan, 2002] and G. Bertuccioli, 'Sinology in Italy 1600–1950', in *Europe Studies China*. London: Hanshang Tang, 1995, pp. 67–78. For the relations between the Roman Empire and the Chinese one, see F. Hirth, *China and the Roman Orient*. Leipzig, 1865; G. Coedès, *Textes d'auteurs Grecs et Latins relatifs à l'Extrême Orient*. Paris, 1910; D. D. Leslie and K. H. J. Gardiner, 'The Roman Empire in Chinese Sources', in *Studi Orientali*, XV, Rome, Università di Roma 'la Sapienza', Dipartimento di Studi Orientali, 1996.

[2] A. C. Moule, *Christians in China before the Year 1550*. London, 1930.

[3] Marco Polo, *Il Milione*, Tuscan version of the Trecento, critical ed. by V. Bertolucci Pizzorusso. Milan, 1975; P. Pelliot, *Notes on Marco Polo*, 3 vols Paris, 1959–73.

[4] The bibliography of missionary activity in China during the XVII and XVIII centuries is vast. See in particular the general works: G. H. Dunne, *Generation of Giants. The Story of the Jesuits in China in the Last Decades of the Ming Dynasty*. London, 1962 and D. E. Mungello, *Curious Land. Jesuit Accomodation and the Ori-*

gins of Sinology. Stuttgart, 1985 and Honolulu, 1989.

[5] An ample bibliography exists for Matteo Ricci: see the works edited by P. Tacchi Venturi, *Opere storichie del P. Matteo Ricci, S.I.*, 2 vols. Macerata, 1913; P. D'Elia, *Fonti Ricciane*. Rome, 1942 (vol. I) and Rome, 1949 (vols II and III); P. D'Elia (edited by), *Il Mappamondo del P. Matteo Ricci S. I.* Vatican City, 1938.

[6] Regarding Giulio Aleni, see in particular the collective volume T. Lippiello and R. Malek (edited by), '*Scholar from the West' Giulio Aleni S.J. (1582–1649) and the Dialogue between Christianity and China*, Monumenta Serica Monograph Series XLII. Nettetal: St. Augustin, 1997.

[7] Regarding Martino Martini, see the first three volumes of *Opera Omnia*, published by the University of Trent, edited by G. Bertuccioli. Trent 1998 (vol. I), Trent 1998 (vol. 2), Trent 2002 (vol. 3, in 2 tomes).

[8] For Filippo Grimaldi, see in particular F. Masini, 'Bio-bibliographical Notes on Claudio Filippo Grimaldi S.J.: Missionary in China (1638–1712)', in N. Forte and F. Masini (edited by), *A Life Journey to the East*. Kyoto, 2002, pp. 185–200.

[9] On the question of the rites, see D. E. Mungello (edited by), *The Chinese Rites Controversy: Its History and Meaning*. Monumenta Serica Institute, Nettetal, St. Augustin and The Ricci Insti-

tute for Chinese Western Cultural History, San Francisco, 1994.

[10] For the history of the relations between the West and China in the XIX century, see J. K. Fairbank, *Trade and Diplomacy on the China Coast. The Opening of the Treaty Ports, 1842–1854*, 2 vols. Harvard (Mass.), 1953; K. Scott Latourette, *A History of Christian Missions in China*. London, 1929; F. Masini, *The Formation of Modern Chinese Lexicon and its Evolution toward a National Language: The Period from 1840 to 1898*, monograph no. 6 of the *Journal of Chinese Linguistics*. Berkeley, University of California, 1993 [Chinese translation: *Xiandai Hanya cihui de xingcheng*. Shanghai, Hanyu da cidian chubanshe, 1997].

[11] Regarding the history of the Collegio in Naples, see M. Fatica and F. D'Arelli (edited by), *La missione cattolica in Cina tra i secoli XVIII-XIX, Matteo Ripa e il Collegio dei Cinesi, Atti del Colloquio Internazionale Napoli 11-12 febbraio 1997*. Naples, Istituto Universitario Orientale, 1999.

[12] F. Masini, 'Different Chinese Perceptions of Europe from Late Ming to Late Qing', in C. Neder, H. Roetz and I. S. Schilling (edited by), *China in seinen biographischen Dimension. Gedenkschrift für Helmut Martin*. Wiesbaden, 2001, pp. 567–75; F. Masini, 'Sino-Western-Japanese Lexical Exchanges in China between the Late Ming and the Late Qing Dynasty', in J. A.

Fogel and J. C. Baxter (edited by), *Historiography and Japanese Consciousness of Value and Norms*. Kyoto, International Research Center for Japanese Studies, 2002, pp. 5–15.

[13] G. Bertuccioli, *Giuseppe Maria Calleri: un piemontese al servizio della Francia in Cina*. Turin, 1986.

[14] G. Bertuccioli, 'Un melodrama incompiuto di Liang Qichao sugli amori di Garibaldi: Xiaqing ji (Storia degli affetti di un eroe)', in G. Borsa and B. Brocchieri (edited by), *Garibaldi, Mazzini e il Risorgimento nel risveglio dell'Asia e dell'Africa*. Milan, 1984, pp. 287–95; G. Bertuccioli, 'A proposito di Garibaldi in Oriente: aprile-settembre 1852', *ibid.*, pp. 417–21.

[15] G. Borsa, *Italia e Cina nel secolo XIX*. Milan, 1961; G. Bertuccioli, 'La prima missione diplomatica cinese in Italia', in *Mondo Cinese*, 3, 1973, pp. 3–13; L. Petech, 'Il primo trattato con l'Italia (1866) nei documenti cinesi', in *Rendiconti, Classe di Scienze Morali*, Accademia Nazionale dei Lincei, XXIX, 1-2, 1974, pp. 17–37.

[16] A. Giovagnoli (edited by), *Roma e Pechino. La svolta extraeuropea di Benedetto XV*. Rome, 1999.

[17] A. S. Lazzarotto, 'Missionario in Cina. L'operazione di Leone Nani nello Shaanxi', in G. Bertuccioli (edited by), *La Cina nelle lastre di Leone Nani (1904-1914)*. Brescia, 1994, pp. 13–18.

The Art

The Missionary Photographer

Roberto Festorazzi

I look again and again at the self-portraits of Leone Nani and the photos portraying him with that strange fixity of his dark eyes. To investigate the mystery of this unique missionary, perhaps more unique than rare, seems to be an undertaking that cannot be taken for granted. What remains is the sensation of not having grasped his more intimate and profound nature. In short, his secret.

For there is something elusive in the dignity of this noble and consummate actor who puts himself on the scene almost like a *pososo*. One might say that there is even a touch of narcissism in this self-referential test of his. And yet, these images—together with his collection of more than 600 plates documenting the China of a century ago—are practically the only things that remain to decipher the enigma of the personality concealed behind the man scrutinising the world through a camera lens. His writings, in fact, do not amount to much for anyone wishing to reconstruct his polyhedral and complex personality, nor has there been much written about him. It is as if an almost derisory destiny were making fun of him. One of the greatest documentary photographers of the twentieth century (because this is what he really was), was content with leaving behind some shots of himself.

Nothing more.

We can only try to make our way through the minefield that discloses a personage who makes life difficult for possible biographers, both present and future.

The documentation conserved at the PIME offers an extraordinary sample of unanswered questions, of interrogatives seeking replies. No spiritual testament exists, letters to family members cannot be found, even his scientific writings seem to be lost for the most part, for example, his studies of officinal plants. In a recent report that Father Giorgio Licini (a PIME fellow brother) wrote that gives some basic information about his life, one reads: 'Father Nani returned to Albino towards the end of 1914. Why? What day exactly? When did he leave China? Did he have photographic material with him? Or did he leave it in Rome or in Milan?'. I do not wish to be misunderstood. After all, no one is to be blamed for the unsuccessful penetrative force of the biographical investigations. It has to do with an entirely different matter. And that is, there is still a great deal of work to do in order to complete the investigation so that the portrait of Leone Nani is not reduced to a simple sketch lacking a concrete analytical content; the most imminent danger being that of concocting a mere legend, a photograph devoid of contrasts and chiaroscuro that fatally eliminates the gradations of colour. This risk is to be avoided at all costs, because there is no doubt whatsoever that the *protagonist* lies behind the *witness*.

Let us then try to look into the life of this very singular man. The son of Luigi Nani, a tinsmith and plumber, Leone was born on 19 August 1880 at Albino, a village in the Val Seriana that today has fifteen thousand inhabitants. His family was originally from Lanzada in Valmalenco, in the heart of that Valtellina that had been the scene of bitter and bloody conflicts between Catholics and the Reformed Church. Leone had two brothers, Giuseppe, he too a tinsmith, and Attilio, who would follow in his brother's footsteps, carrying out for many years his mission as a priest in a Roman parish, and one sister, Felicita. Valtellinese tenacity along with a certain peasant impulse that was as picturesque as it was sagacious made up the inner stuff accompanying Nani on his unusual missionary adventure. Leone was a year older than Angelo Roncalli, another man from Bergamo whose travels led him far in his lifetime. He encountered disastrous and persistent incomprehension until, as a young priest 'in the odour of modernism', he became secretary to a good and enlightened bishop, Monsignor Giacomo Maria Radini Tedeschi.[1]

Even the extroverted and congenial nature of Leone Nani procured the owner of such a head and heart diverse headaches. 'Don Allegro', as he came to be called at times by those close to him, and as he later signed himself on the writings he sent from the land of his mission, was not always that. At Albino, his sacerdotal vocation had already emerged precociously so that Leone was directed to the Episcopal seminary in Bergamo. His report card at the end of this second year of secondary school[2] documents a significant inclination for scientific subjects and, at the same time, points out the features of a divergent personality, one of great intellectual vivacity destined to explore new worlds more than digest the *latinorum*. His highest marks (apart from a nine in religion) were two eights in Natural History and French, followed by sevens in Italian and Ancient History, and just passing marks of six in Greek and Latin.

But while the boy's call to the priesthood was recognised by everyone, Nani ran into tenacious resistance when he announced his missionary vocation. The documents in our possession attest that the 'turning point' in his life occurred during his eighteenth year. Nani was probably impatient with seminarian discipline, because the vocation 'hatching' inside of him was not at all favoured by his teachers. On 20 September 1898, the Bergamasque boy entered the Pontificio Seminario dei Santi Apostoli Pietro e Paolo in Rome. His vocation was

encouraged and supported by Monsignor Federico Gambarelli, at the time the rector of the Albino sanctuary of Nostra Signora di Guadalupe. It is interesting to note in this regard that Reverend Gambarelli had, to his credit, a rather unusual background: in fact, he did not become a priest until he was 40, after having abandoned an artistic career as a tenor that had reached the highest peaks and international fame.

At any rate, Nani's entry into the Roman seminary was hardly 'pacific'. We learn from some documents of that period, for example, that some Bergamo priests, having recognised the good qualities of Nani's slightly rebellious character, followed his evolution in trepidation. Nani literally escaped from the Bergamo seminary, followed it seems by the fame of the disciplinary remarks made against him. Indeed, his childhood teachers, that is, those who knew him best, rushed to his aid. Don Alberto Casari, who signed as an 'eighty-year old priest', sent a grief-stricken letter to the rector in Rome on 26 November 1898 begging him not to use a strong hand with the eighteen-year old, a victim of 'so many useless and unjust altercations'.[3] The venerable priest implored God that Leone, after having strayed from the straight and narrow path, 'be returned to the path of an ecclesiastical career' and begged 'the Lord and the Virgin' (and perhaps the rector of the Roman seminary more than anyone else) to help the boy 'and preserve him in his sincere repentance'. The good Don Casari concluded his letter by appealing to his interlocutor: 'I recommend him to your personal charity in order that you correct him and advise him if necessary'.

Even Don Battista Peroni drew up a declaration of his own attesting to the young man's good qualities; a declaration that has no value, however, *erga omnes*, because he who wrote it pointed out that it is not destined 'for the Monsignor Bishop or the rector of the seminary of Bergamo',[4] but for 'superiors at other institutes'.

In Rome, the decision to send Nani to China was probably an almost obligatory one; indeed, the Pontificio Seminario dei Santi Apostoli Pietro e Paolo—which joined the Seminario Lombardo per le Missioni Estere in 1926 becoming today's PIME—had its own mission at Hanzhong in Shaanxi. In those days, there were very few missions founded by the missionary institute. Shortly after his ordination as a priest on 6 June 1903, Father Leone Nani departed for China. It was 20 September 1903 and the young priest could not help but feel a bit unsettled at the idea of the new life awaiting him. He wrote down his feelings in a kind of diary during his voyage to the East, in the form of a letter addressed to the rector of his institute: 'I always tried to be happy; but every now and then I had a lump in my throat; it was a hiccup that nature wrenched from the bottom of my soul. You can imagine what my thoughts were at that moment… the silent greeting that broke out of my heart was a warm, melancholy goodbye, the first and perhaps the last that I made to Italy, my birthplace, to my desolate relatives, to my dear superiors and fond companions at the Seminary…'.[5]

Not long after, the nostalgia on leaving his dear ones gave way to his innate curiosity and strong spirit of observation, and he described all the places he saw during his journey in great detail: 'From the deck, Port Said has the appearance of a lovely strip of land that gradually stretches out to the sea where it is lapped by calm waves. Some of the gardens on view have been cultivated by delicate hands and make one think that in that small palace with ancient crenellations, or in the other one with a Turkish terrace, some quite civilised family must live'.[6] And further: 'Here is the Sinai… here is the Sinai…. It rose up from down there like some enormous cliff, perhaps red-hot from the burning sun. A small cloud that rose lightly from the foaming waves and went to perch on the holy mountain… however the thunder was missing… the lightning… Moses and the Tables of the Law, otherwise it would be possible to bring that famous page of the Bible back to life'.[7]

The first photographs that portray Nani in China, probably taken shortly after his arrival, depict him before his external metamorphosis. The young priest from Albino still wears the priest's cassock, but has let his thick beard grow. A curious image, one difficult to date, represents him instead in civilian clothes: a wrinkled, oversized jacket, and a black broad-brimmed hat that together with the beard and oval spectacles give him a professorial look.

From the very beginning, while he busied himself studying Chinese along with his companion Father Checchi in the residence of Guluba, Nani made an effort to become familiar with that land and those people.

It was not until the spring of 1905, when another group of missionaries arrived in China from Italy, that he could finally work on his own in the town of Yangxian on the Han river. After having accompanied an older fellow brother for some time, Father Nani assumed direct responsibility for the entire district, which extended to the slopes of the Qin Ling Mountains. A young and enterprising missionary, Father Nani did not spare himself in his peregrinations, and in addition to his work of evangelisation and the administration of the sacraments, he also saw to the construction of chapels and residences. During his long journeys, he carefully observed the habits, customs and details of everyday life, often fixing them on his extraordinary plates.

Some two years after his arrival in the Celestial Empire, there was a significant change in Father Nani's own appearance, indicating an advanced process of 'Sinicization'. In homage to the local custom, for example, he wore the Manchu pigtail. A photograph of him at a baptism shows him with a stole draped over a long white *changpao* gown with a *jijin* cap on his head, the latter being an accessory that the Catholic priests used during liturgical ceremonies from 1615 to 1924.

That the missionary Nani had contracted a kind of 'China sickness' can be demonstrated by the way he observes and documents the reality before his eyes on his photographic plates and in his writings. His reports on the manufacture of bamboo paper, 'postal chimneys', cormorant fishing, the abolition of opium and the elimination of the Manchu pigtail attest to the missionary's vast cultural and scientific interests. At times his descriptions, albeit always attentive and precise, take on a lively, amused tone: for example, the report accompanying and commenting his detailed photographic reportage of the original method of cultivating the so-called 'ear mushrooms'. 'Among the disparate, undisputable and really Oriental tastes of the "children of heaven" for certain dishes and sauces is their predilection for a kind of mushroom that tempts and satisfies the Chinese palate. The mushroom that I'm talking about, commonly called "muërz", that is, "ear of wood" or "ear mushroom", among the Chinese, holds the primate over all other common mushrooms…'.[8] Other times instead, his style is purely descriptive and encyclopaedic, as when Nani talks about *Corydalis Cornutus*, a kind of coleopteran that he had discovered in the mountains of Fwayang: 'This large insect could be said to share some of the characteristics of the coleopterans, hymenopterans and butterflies. It is about fourteen centimetres long. The male has a large, hard head with four little horns like thorns; it is of a black colour speckled and variegated in red. It has two big amber eyes on the sides and two other smaller ones almost united on top of its head, not far from two long filiform antenna…'.[9]

Nonetheless, without belittling the written texts, Nani's photographs are really what should be observed with attention. A propos of this, I do have a sneaking suspicion that behind the absolute perfection of so many images, from the landscapes to the scenes of daily life, there may be hidden a deception or possible equivocation. The apex of formal elegance reached by Nani leads one to think that the repertoire he handed down may only partially respond to the canons of pure documentary work, which are concerned solely with transposing a slice of reality into images, albeit mediated by the subjectivity of the man portraying it. There is, in short, an attempt here to 'direct' segments of Chinese life and culture in an almost theatrical way. His scenic sense is at a maximum, for example, in the photograph in which Nani repeats his fall from a horse. The original idea behind the image seems to have been that of describing Father Nani's misadventure to his family. But the 'freeze frame' effect is irresistible, because with one single shot impressed on the plate, he managed to transmit the entire sequence marvellously, not only with an impressive 'ethnic' set, but also with his extraordinary skill as a director.

In another case, Nani signed one of his works like the great Alfred Hitchcock, by peeping out of the tiny window of a thatched-roof hovel: the detail might escape a superficial look for his face is barely visible, being off to one side with respect to the centre of the scene. That Nani was a great director is further documented by the photographs in which his attire is anything but that of a placid Catholic priest.

The photographs of our missionary with a Chinese pigtail, shaven head and dressed in Mandarin-style Chinese outfits have thus been left to the almost inevitable destiny of posthumous rediscovery.

The symbolism that often emerges in Nani's portraiture is reminiscent of the stylistic features of the painting of a fellow countryman, Giovan Battista Moroni,[10] the great innovator of figurative art in Italy during the Counter-Reformation. It is impossible to know if and how much Moroni's 'lesson' influenced Nani's artistic development, but the analogies are certainly noteworthy. Inspired by a northern, Flemish conception of painting that he came into contact with during his long permanence in Trent during the years of the Council, Moroni, whose works are now to be found in the leading museums of the world, sought to create an ideal type of portraiture. Intended as a celebrative confirmation of a class ethic, it was cultivated and naturalistic and displayed a sensitive psychological understanding of his figures: in short, a 'moral portrait' of clear didactic intent.

Nor is there in Nani's photographs any trace of *epos*, something that might be expected from a missionary who had arrived in China.

The arduous working conditions in which the Catholic missionaries found themselves during the difficult period of transition from the Empire to the Republic required a prudence that did not permit any satisfied trace of triumphalism. Further, the political protection exercised over the Catholic missionaries by the foreign powers (*in primis*, France), whose interests in China were hardly compatible with Christian charity, weighed heavily on the presence and work of the evangelisers.

The reason why Leone Nani returned from China in 1914 is not known. His sudden repatriation has never been clarified, and the excuse of the missionary's presumed illness (malaria?) has never been documented. An elderly relative of Father Leone, Felice Nani, who still lives in Albino, suggests that the priest may have had to leave China because of 'a clash of political nature with the Chinese ambience'. But, here too, no objective verification exists.

However that may be, on his return to Italy, Nani was sent to a military hospital where he gave spiritual assistance: the First World War had broken out in Europe. At the end of the conflict, he went back to being a diocesan priest in Albino, where he taught Latin to the seminarians at the Apostolic School of the Sacred Heart. In 1922, he was assigned to the little church of the Santissima Trinità, situated a few kilometres from the centre of Albino, on the other side of the Serio river. He continued his pastoral work in that countryside, and is still remembered by many today. In Albino, Nani would occasionally come out with something in Chinese, and he never lost his love for riding. He devoted himself to the young, involving them in a variety of amusing activities. During the novena in preparation for the Feast of the Santissima Trinità, Father Leone (who, in the meantime, had returned to the title of 'Don') sent the youngsters out in search of snails. Their empty shells were filled with oil so that they could be used as tiny lamps, which were then placed on the steps leading up to the church.

Nani also managed to set up a cinema at the church. On warm summer evenings, he would hang a large white sheet across the church façade and then project many of his photographs from China on it, and, it seems, even some movies made with the very first movie cameras.

On 8 May 1935, at the age of 55, Father Leone had a heart attack during a train journey to Milan. When he got off the train at the station of Lambrate, he suffered a cardiac crisis, and it was impossible to save his life. The aim of this last journey had been to help the Sacred Heart seminarians set up a small power station.

An impressive procession wound through the streets of Albino during his funeral which was celebrated on 11 May. A newspaper article in the *Eco di Bergamo* reported the following day: 'A grandiose, moving and unforgettable display of mourning was to be seen at the funeral of the lamented Reverend Father Leone Nani. The memory of Father Nani will not fade away very easily from the souls of the Albino people. With him passes away the beautiful and saintly figure of a Priest and Missionary'.

He now rests in the cemetery of the town where 'Don Allegro' first opened his eyes onto the world.

[1] Cf. J. L. Gonzáles-Balado, *Il cuore di Papa Giovanni*. Rome: PIME, 2002.

[2] Report card of the scholastic year 1895–96, Rome, PIME General Archive, title XXIII, vol. 10. fol. 1009.

[3] Letter from Albino of 26 November 1898, Rome, PIME General Archive, title XXIII, vol. 10, fol. 1006.

[4] Letter from Albino of 12 October 1898, Rome, PIME General Archive, title XXIII, vol. 10, fol. 1003.

[5] Letter of Father Leone Nani from Port Said, 25 September 1903, published in *Bollettino del Seminario*, year 1903, p. 137.

[6] Letter of Father Leone Nani from Gibuti, 6 October 1903, published in *Bollettino del Seminario*, year 1903, pp. 162–63.

[7] *Ibid.*, p. 164.

[8] Rome, PIME General Archive, title XXIII, vol. 10, fol. 1051.

[9] Rome, PIME General Archive, title XXIII, vol. 10, fol. 1149.

[10] See in this regard the two-volume work *Storia delle terre di Albino*. Brescia: Grafo edizioni, 1996.

China in Photography between the Eighteenth and Nineteenth Centuries

Lionello Lanciotti

The Chinese love to use the words *lao zhaopian* (or 'old photographs') when they refer to their photographic heritage. It is therefore not surprising that the same term was adopted as the title for a series of volumes that began to be published in China in 1997 with a circulation of thirty thousand copies and a periodic frequency of four to five issues per year. It is only recently that the Chinese have begun to publish books dedicated to these kinds of images, but the aforementioned series is only one of the many regarding the historic photos of the most important cities or significant quarters. One example is the beautiful volume *Beijing Lao Tianqiao* (Tianqiao of Old Peking), which appeared in 1990 and is dedicated to the ancient Pekinese quarter situated near the Heavenly Altar, where jugglers, tumblers, acrobats and actors perform in the street. One might say that a kind of fashion has begun, and everyone everywhere has been digging up material to be published from family and town archives. It is what an Italian scholar, Federico Greselin, has accurately described in his essay, as the 'literature of memory'. Photography reached China, introduced by the Westerners, in the second half of the nineteenth century. It was really an undertaking to photograph in those far-off years. The photos were made on glass plates, and it was necessary to carry a large quantity of them; further, spare parts as well as the chemicals required for developing were needed; pure water was absolutely indispensable, something not often available *in loco*, as was a

good supply of fresh eggs, since albumin was necessary for the glass plates. A famous Scottish photographer, John Thomson, who worked in China between 1868 and 1872, recounts in his book that 'he took delight in being famed as a dangerous geomancer, because it was believed that my camera was a mysterious black object that enabled me to see through rocks and mountains, to penetrate inside the genuine souls of the people and produce marvellous images, thanks to a kind of black magic'.[1] In another work, the same photographer writes that 'in order to transport the baggage, an escort of eight to ten porters was necessary' and he also remembers how 'the photographs had to be prepared and developed at the place, with this advantage: the negatives could be examined immediately, retouched and packed in the baggage'.[2]

The first photographers were authentic professionals. One cannot help but remember that among the first was a great Venetian photographer, Felice Beato, who may be called the first war photo-reporter. Born around 1834, he died in Burma in 1907 (or 1908), and after becoming a British citizen, he changed his name from Felice to Felix. A photo-journalist during the Crimean War, he later went to India where he photographed scenes of the famous anti-British uprising, the Great Mutiny of 1857. In 1860, the second Opium War broke out in China, which saw a combined French and English army fighting the Imperial Chinese forces. Beato followed the Western troops as an accredited photographer, shooting not only war scenes, but also the famous Summer Palace, the *Yuan Ming Yuan*, that was barbarously destroyed and sacked shortly thereafter by the Anglo-French troops. We are also indebted to his camera for the oldest photos of the wall and gates of Peking, most of which was knocked down during the 1950s. He also made some remarkable portraits such as that of Prince Gong, the Manchu emperor's brother. An Englishman who had witnessed the taking of this photograph, Henry Knollys, writes that when 'Beato aimed the large lens of his camera in the direction of the chest of the unhappy Prince Gong…, the latter looked up in a state of terror, as pale as a dead man'.[3] The prince's photograph was the very first photographic portrait to be taken in China.

That one of the first photographers in China was an Italian is good reason to be proud. Felice Beato, whose works have been shown in numerous exhibitions both in Italy and abroad, was a restless man, driven more by curiosity and adventure than by a desire for material gain; he wandered from Eastern Europe to the Near Eastern countries, from India to China, from Japan, where he lived and worked for some ten years, to Burma. His 102 photographs portraying aspects of China at the time of the second Opium War represent a precious documentation of that particular historical moment.

Not long before the short but significant sojourn of Felice Beato in China, an English company with the apparently Italian firm name of Negretti & Zambra opened an office in Canton (1858), entrusting its direction to a French photographer, Monsieur Dossier. During the latter half of the nineteenth century, many French, English and Italian photographers set out for China in order to take photos that they hoped to be able to sell in the West, where anything that could be described as exotic was becoming more and more fashionable. It was not easy, however, to set up a studio in China without considerable financial support. Many photographers literally went bankrupt and their material ended up for the most part at 'The Firm', a company founded in the late 1960s in Hong Kong by a couple of wandering photographers, Weed and Howard. The photographic materials of some eleven studios that had operated between 1860 and 1877 and gone bankrupt were collected by the two and the

company managers who followed them; they supplied photos of China as well as of other Far Eastern Asian countries throughout the latter part of the nineteenth century to anyone who wished to purchase them.

The name of the Scottish John Thomson (1837–1921), one of the greatest pioneers of Western photography in China together with Felice Beato, has already been mentioned. However, while the latter limited himself primarily to documenting Peking and its surroundings, Thomson, who also supplied the *China Magazine* of Hong Kong with photographs, carried out his work in many areas of central and northern China, during the journeys he made between 1868 and 1872. Not satisfied simply with photographing landscapes and monuments, he also immortalised the common people and those belonging to the upper classes, thus supplying the Western public with a real picture of what China was like in the last quarter of the nineteenth century. Some ten of his books, which appeared in London during the last decades of the century, collected and divulged several hundreds of his best photographs. Unfortunately, it is not possible to remember the names of all the leading photographers who worked in China at the turn of the century. Many Western museums possess heterogeneous material, from that produced by scientific expeditions to that of simple amateurs. The Musée Guimet in Paris, one of the most important European museums of Asian art, conserves more than five thousand photos on plates, the fruit of travels in China on the part of such famous sinologists as Edouard Chavannes, Paul Pelliot and Victor Segalen. That same museum also owns the numerous plates of a French diplomat, August François. Further, there have been many publications and exhibitions of these collections. Recently (2001–2), the Musée Départemental Albert-Kahn of Boulogne-Billancourt published two large volumes containing 2108 photographs commissioned by the banker Albert Kahn between 1909 and 1934.

From a technical point of view, an authentic revolution began when reasonably sized cameras and film substituted glass plates. The photographic art was no longer the monopoly of a few professionals, and passed into the hands of amateurs, some of whom managed to obtain more than satisfactory results. This was the case of Donald Mennie, a businessman who arrived in China in 1899 and published a magnificent book in folio in 1920 entitled *The Pageant of Peking*, with 66 photogravures that represent the most suggestive images of the Chinese capital at the beginning of the twentieth century.

Between 1900 and 1901, Giuseppe Messerotti Benvenuti was present in China; as a soldier he had been part of the Italian contingent sent to participate in the repression of the Boxer rebellion. An amateur photographer, he used what he loved to refer to as a 'little box camera bought in Naples', an original portable Kodak of Eastman Kodak & Co. His snapshots were recently discovered in a family archive and published (Modena, 2000).

A short time later, Father Leone Nani arrived in China. That Lombard missionary would remain there for ten years, and with two plate cameras, one 13 × 18 and the other 9 × 12, would amuse himself by taking a vast number of splendid photographs whose negatives, about 640, are today conserved in the Milanese archives of the Pontifical Institute for Foreign Missions (PIME). Father Leone Nani had come to China with a good preparation in sinology and experience in photography, so that he was able to choose his subjects with competence. In 1994, the Foundation 'Civiltà Bresciana' published a volume containing a number of the wonderful photographs taken by him. One of its editors was the sinologist, Giuliano Bertuccioli, the author of an excellent essay on Father Nani.

[1] J. Thomson, *Illustrations of China and Its People*. London: Sampson Low, Marston, Pearle, 1873–74.
[2] J. Thomson, *Through China with a Camera*, 2nd ed. London: 1898.
[3] H. Knollys, *Incidents in the China War of 1860*. Edinburgh and London: W. Blackwood and Sons, 1875, pp. 209–10.

Bibliography
P. Battaglia, N. Labanca (edited by), *Giuseppe Messerotti Benvenuti, un italiano nella Cina dei Boxer (1900-1901)*. Modena: Associazione G. Panini, 2000.

E. Boerschmann, *Old China in Historic Photographs*. New York: Dover Press, 1982.
L. Carrington Goodrich, *The Face of China as Seen by Photographers and Travelers 1860–1912*. New York: Aperture Inc., 1978.
F. Greslin, *Vecchie fotografie cinesi come stimolo e pretesto per una letteratura della memoria*, in 'Quaderni dell'Amicizia', 3 (2001), Associazione Italia-Cina, Rome, pp. 21-37.
D. Harris, *Of Battle and Beauty. Felice Beato's Photographs of China*. Santa Barbara: Museum of Art, 1999.
Hu Zhichuan and Chen Shen, *A Collection of Early-Period Chinese Photographs (1840-1919)*.

Beijing: The China Photography Publishing House, 1987.
L. Lanciotti, 'Vecchie Foto di Cina: tentativo di una bibliografia', in *Cina*, 24 (1993), IsMEO, pp. 171–73.
L. Lanciotti, 'Agli albori della fotografia occidentale in Cina', in *Quaderni dell'Amicizia*, 3 (2001), Associazione Italia-Cina, pp. 11–20.
J. Thomson, *Illustrations of China and Its People*, 4 vols. London: Sampson Low, Marston, Pearle, 1873.
C. Worswich & Jonathan Spence, *Imperial China. Photographs 1850-1912*. London: Scholar Press, 1979.

Notes sur quelques photographies de la Chine au XIX siécle à l'occasion de l'exposition 'La Chine entre le collodion humide & la gélatinobromure'. Paris: Bibliothèque Nationale, 1979.
Chine/China 1909-1934. Catalogue of the Photographs and Film Sequences from the Musée Albert-Kahn, 2 vols. Boulogne-Billancourt: Musée Départemental Albert-Kahn, 2001–2.

Mysteries of a Reporter

Giovanna Calvenzi

I saw Father Nani's photographs for the first time at the end of the 1980s. Sandro Girella, the owner of a photography agency, had brought a selection of images of China from the beginning of the century to the editorial office of *Sette*, the *Corriere della Sera* supplement for which I was then working. The author was unknown to us, but the extraordinary quality of the material revealed it to be the work of an exceptional photographer. In 1994, while preparing the volume *La Cina nelle lastre di Leone Nani*,[1] I worked on the Nani archive for a second time. On that occasion I tried to reconstruct, thanks to the generous contribution of Father Mario Marazzi, then the director of the Museo Popoli e Culture del PIME of Milan and the Institute archives, the figure of Father Nani, missionary and photographer, seeking to place him in the traditional area of the photographers-travellers, the pioneers of photography in the second half of the nineteenth century, to which Nani had every right to belong. I then approached Nani's work for the third time, presuming to know a great deal and, almost certain of knowing his archive, able to make a critical analysis of his work. The circa 640 plates that he left us are not many and although exceptional, so I told myself, seeing them again would add little to what I thought I already knew. In order to find a different interpretative viewpoint, I therefore decided to consult his contact prints, that is, all those made from the plates of his photographic fund. For insiders, contact prints are a privileged instrument for learning about a photographer's ability as well as his personality. There is no censorship in contact prints, nor are there changes of mind; everything that has been photographed is there, be it good or bad. In Nani's case, however, I realised that his contact prints were the victim of a structural flaw: it was not the author himself who had put the negatives in the order he wanted according to his own intentions, but rather some other person after him who arranged the images he had left.

A quick first look confirmed the extraordinary efficacy and modernity of Nani's narration. At the time of his departure for China, photography was exactly seventy-five years old: on calculating time by the speed of evolution marking the recent decades, it is a lot, but when one considers the rhythm of change and the discoveries of the second half of the nineteenth century, then it is a relatively brief period of time. As a pioneer, Nani certainly had to work with instruments that were heavy and difficult to transport, ones that required physical gifts as well as a technical-scientific competence that contemporary photographers can ignore. Not only. Nani worked in an area of China that was far from centres of communication, an area, as he himself put it, that was 'perennially damp', and not particularly favourable for practising photography or finding additional plates or spare parts for his cameras.

As a whole, his contact prints reveal a great technical mastery of the means, a remarkable talent for composition and, generally speaking, an attitude of generous curiosity towards whatever he saw and photographed. However, one also wants to know more, to understand what led Nani to devote himself to this photographic documentation along with his missionary work, which certainly had priority and was marked by danger and hard work.

'Confined between 1904 and 1914 to the interior of China, where the strength of tradition still made itself heard, Father Nani was able to record with his camera the last transformations he was able to observe'. Thus wrote Giuiliano Bertuccioli in the introduction to the above-mentioned book. An impeccable analysis: to be at the centre of such dramatic events is certainly a reason for wanting to document them, but this is only a partial answer and does not fully explain the reasons for doing that work and, above all, his way of working. After seeing the contact prints, I decided to look into the abundant correspondence left by Nani.

The description of his sea voyage to the mission portrays a twenty-three year old who is curious, open, and fears neither the forces of nature nor physical discomfort. He jokes with his travelling companions, ironises about the dangers they have survived, and every now and then drops a small gem that reveals more about the culture he grew up in than about his character. He sees veiled Arab women at the Gibuti port of call, 'with a ribbon or a white bone at the mouth' commenting: 'Oh, if only there were some of that reservedness among European women!'. He writes with vivacity, recounting anecdotes about the journey and describing the people and the landscapes, but does not think about himself very much or what awaits him in China.

When faced with the discomforts, heat and stench of Gibuti, he expresses an opinion, perhaps the only one, regarding photography: 'A snapshot could give a much more accurate picture of this indigenous life than any vivid description, and it is worth being reproduced by one of our cinematographers so as to spare the curious the trouble of coming here to see it for themselves'.

This humorous observation confusing cinema and photography would suggest that Nani thinks that the documentation of places should serve as a means for avoiding distasteful experiences. He never hints in the letters or reports written during his voyage at the important role photography would play in his life in the subsequent ten years.

It was at this point that I realised that the writings and the contact prints delineated the same person. Nani photographs as he writes and, probably, as he lives: with simplicity, curiosity, energy, and an insuppressible vitality.

Nani practices all types of photography with total naturalness. His posed portraits anticipate the documentary style and methodology of August Sander and Walker Evans,[2] great masters who would work some decades later. He devotes himself to architecture, landscape and still life with a limpid rigorous vision. He takes on reportage by photographing papermaking, cormorant fishing, and the construction of the new church in the Vicariate of Hanzhong in a series of impeccable narrative sequences. Both his interpretative ability and commitment are decidedly professional. It has been for long asked, albeit in vain, where he learned to photograph, develop negatives and make prints. One may ask what he knew about the other photographers who had been in China before him,[3] but all this does nothing but lengthen the list of answerless questions. The bulk of his production is devoted to portraits. His compositions show that he put into practice the teachings of the 'photography studios' of his time, which had opened all over the world and which for technical and cultural reasons had created a specific type of portrait.

The Fratelli Alinari Studio, to mention an Italian one, opened in Florence in 1852 and, in addition to photographs of cities and works of art, specialised in portraits, a genre that was then extremely popular and in demand. The Studio had a variety of elegant settings where subjects who wished to be photographed would pose in their best clothes. Their poses were static, their eyes glued to the camera, and the image itself revealed the many details of the setting that the client had chosen. Father Nani manages to recreate a veritable photographic studio with what he has on hand. He uses a neutral or richly decorated background in order to isolate his models from their environmental context, supplying them with European clocks, spittoons, flower vases, and simple or inlaid chairs. In any case, his attention to the composition and his respect for physiognomies and costumes construct a mosaic that reveals a profound anthropological interest and therefore furnishes a kind of 'catalogue' of the human typologies in China at the turn of the twentieth century. But his contribution is even greater, for he offers the more attentive observer further elements that reveal a creative freshness.

In the formally impassive compositions, Nani gives a wink of his eye and a wry smile appears on his lips: the two newlyweds have unexpectedly crossed their legs as if they were hinting at a polite form of intimacy; a stern-faced soldier uses a safety pin to keep his collar closed; the Chinese dignitaries are wearing European hats… However, the self-portraits may supply a possible key for interpreting the mystery behind the photographer Nani. Although self-portraits were not a standard practice even then (the first, made by Hippolyte Bayard[4] dates back to 1840), Father Nani's intention of portraying himself most likely has nothing to do with any form of exhibitionism, and is probably much closer to his need 'to document'. For him, photography is an instrument that enables him to exercise his not indifferent scientific knowledge, innate curiosity and ability to command in any situation. Nani shows himself during his stay in China with a pigtail or a beard, wearing a priest's cassock or Chinese clothing, with a rifle or a camera, alone or with Chinese officials, on horseback or as he has fallen off, with a pipe or an explorer's hat, while he playfully peeks out of a house window or listens severely to a catechism exam. It is his serious face that raises a suspicion: his expression never changes, be the situation humorous or surreal, as if his photographic work were nothing but a funny joke, a polite irreverence to inform and amuse those looking at his photos. The committed and devoted missionary shows himself to be 'Don Allegro' in the photographs, that boy with mischievous eyes who is full of life notwithstanding his impassive expression. The same curiosity, the same spirit of lightness with which he most likely handled the problems of his apostolate are also to be found in the images that today are considered reportage. Everything seems to interest him and in order to fully achieve what was probably a didactic-informative preoccupation of his, he does not hesitate to pose his subjects, taking care to direct each situation, once again the forerunner of a working method that has recently provoked a great deal of discussion and reflection as to the truth or veracity of photography. Naturally, Nani does not create any problems for himself: he witnesses the execution of a convict sentenced to death with journalistic rigour just as he does nuptial or funeral processions, circus work or peasants eating, and he gets fishermen, miners and papermakers to pose for him while still conserving the 'true' immediacy of the narration.

There is another observation in one of his writings, dedicated to the new church of an Italian Vicariate,[5] that may offer further information about the photographer Father Nani: 'Indeed, by themselves the word and life that the missionary sacrifices simply do not have the lasting suggestive force to win the hearts of these Chinese who only live by appearances and profound pagan superstitions, but it is still useful to conquer them initially with external attractions, ingratiating and teasing their innate curiosity so that they may be led to learn something in matters of religion and to an initial belief and faith in it'.

Did photography also have in Nani's apostolate those ingratiating and teasing characteristics of external attraction that made it possible for him to come even closer to such a different people?

Everything leads one to think that in Nani's relationship with photography that too was present: the use of a creative instrument to come closer to his new interlocutors, to fascinate and involve them, a means to amuse himself and others, yet always and everywhere performing the twofold role of documenting and informing.

This hypothesis would also respond to the queries raised regarding Nani's total disinterest towards photography on his return to Italy. Once his mandate had expired, he may have found new interests and certainly new complications at home, and the precious instrument that he made use of to teach us to see China at the beginning of the century was set aside without a second thought.

[1] G. Bertuccioli (edited by), *La Cina nelle lastre di Leone Nani (1904-1914)*. Milan: PIME, 1994 (vol. I), 1999 (vol. II).

[2] In the interim between the two world wars August Sander (1876–1964) published *Citizens of the Twentieth Century*, an impressive series of portraits that present a kind of visual encyclopaedia of the German nation. Walker Evans (1903–75) collaborated on an American government project between 1935 and 1938 that documented living conditions in some agricultural areas of the United States. Both are considered outstanding representatives of what has been called the 'documentary style'.

[3] For information regarding how many were working in China before Father Leone Nani, see the essay by Lionello Lanciotti, in this volume.

[4] Hippolyte Bayard was the unfortunate inventor of the negative-positive system. A few days after the announcement of the invention of the daguerreotype at the Academy of Sciences in 1839, he tried to obtain a patent for his process, but was silenced with a modest pension. In order to emphasise his difficulties as an inventor, Bayard then came up with a provocative self-portrait: himself as a cadaver, namely *Self-portrait as a Drowned Man*, 1840.

[5] Rome, PIME General Archive, title XXIII, vol. 10, fol. 1043.

The Photographs

Self-portraits

A generous and enterprising missionary, Father Leone Nani was also an acute observer of every aspect of daily life in China. During the ten years of his apostolate he travelled far and wide throughout the region of Shaanxi, and immortalised with his camera, on plates of an extraordinary evocative power, the habits, customs, landscapes, natural wealth and misery of the people.

For the PIME missionary, photography was an instrument of knowledge that enabled him not only to satisfy his innate curiosity, but also to implement one of his tasks: that of sending back to Italy an illustrated account of his mission. His images, which respond to the needs of his apostolate, are not, however, the mere fruit of a duty, but rather of an instinct and desire to share an experience of learning and to penetrate into that faraway world, so as to thoroughly understand—and make understood—such a different social reality.

Responding to this need are also numerous self-portraits and these may provide us with a key to interpreting the mystery of the photographer Nani. Here too, the missionary's intention to pose presumably had nothing to do with any form of exhibitionism, but instead was closer to a need to 'document' by showing himself in the different situations that arose in his apostolate as well as his gradual approach to local customs.

The 'Western' Nani who had just arrived in China, dressed in a priest's cassock, soon turned into a missionary garbed in Chinese clothing, while his beard was substituted by the typical pigtail of the Manchu period. We see him immortalised with a rifle, attesting to the many dangers that the missionary ran into those days, but also with his great passion, the camera. Many of the portraits are posed—alone or together with Chinese dignitaries or his fellow priests—but there are also numerous, amusing scenes of life, with Nani, who has stopped for refreshment during a peregrination, or on horseback, or even in a carefully studied reproduction of a fall.

Nani narrates himself with the same vivacity and creativity with which he photographs the people and life of the place and with the same attention to detail. We see him with a pipe or an explorer's hat, severely listening to catechism exams or playfully peering out of a window, almost as if he wished to 'sign' that plate with his fleeting appearance.

Endowed with a remarkable scientific background and a great capacity to command in any situation, Father Nani uses photography as an instrument to document the diverse aspects of Chinese life of the time as well as his own personal experience as a missionary in China.

Thus, in addition to the technical quality and beauty of the photos, Nani's work is to be recognised for its extraordinary historical-documentary value. His is not only a unique testimony of the missionary epoch, of which he was one of the protagonists, but above all of a world, the Chinese one of those years that was far from being concerned about the visual documentation of its own social heritage, its customs and its work.

Self-portraits

1.
Father Nani at 23 years of age, probably on his arrival in China.

2.
*Self-portrait of Father Nani with a long Chinese gown (*changshan*) and his inseparable camera, the faithful companion that enabled him to document many aspects of Chinese life of the time.*

3.
Group portrait: Father Nani with teachers and students.

4.
Group of missionaries: Father Nani is the first on the lower left.

5.
Father Nani at Hankow, perhaps on his arrival in China. He still wears the Roman cassock.

6.
Father Nani with a hunting rifle.

7.
Father Nani with some collaborators at the mission. An example of cultural exchange: the missionary wears an Oriental hat and clothing, while the three Chinese wear European hats.

8.
Self-portrait of Father Nani.

9.
Like all the missionaries of his time, Father Nani also adopted Chinese clothing and local customs. In this self-portrait he wears the majia *over a long gown (*changshan*) as well as the pigtail imposed on the Chinese by their Manchu rulers.*

10.
Father Nani portrayed next to the piano
as he listens to a fellow priest play.

11.
Father Nani at the table as he eats a typically Chinese meal, but with Western cutlery.

13.
Missionaries posing. Father Nani is standing in the centre, Monsignor Passerini is the second from the left.

14.
Maurizio Bensa, in white in the centre, the interpreter of the Italian Legation in Peking, during a visit to the Italian missions in Hanzhong in July 1910. Monsignor Passerini is on his left.

15.
*Father Nani baptising a group of babies.
He wears the* jijin *on his head that Catholic
priests used in liturgical ceremonies until
1924.*

Self-portraits

16.
Self-portrait in a long Chinese outfit.
17.
Father Nani in Mandarin dress.

18.
Father Nani in front of a church, probably at Guluba.

19.
Self-portrait on a horse with a groom.

20.
A meal on the road, during one of Father Nani's many apostolic peregrinations.

21.
*Father Nani during a catechism exam
at Chekiading.*

22.
*Fall from a horse. A genre scene in which
Father Nani simulates an accident that most
probably really happened.*

Self-portraits

Between the Empire and the Republic

The last imperial dynasty to rule in China, from 1644 to 1911, was that of the Qing, founded by the Manchu, a barbarian population of the north. With the era of Qianlong (second half of the eighteenth century), the Qing dynasty reached its greatest power, ruling over the most extensive territory that a Chinese sovereign had ever possessed. But already by the last years of the eighteenth century the signs of decline of this great Empire were to be noted: in fact, the class of officials, whose economy was based on large landed estates, soon showed that it could not keep up with the rapidly changing situation. Further, the Empire, having become a hegemonic power in all of Eastern Asia, began to attract the interest of the Europeans who, beginning with Father Matteo Ricci (in China from 1583 until the time of his death in 1610) through the Jesuits and other missionaries to travellers and merchants, had developed a greater and more precise knowledge of the country.

The profound cultural and political crisis into which China fell was a result of its economic weakness. After the Opium Wars (1839–42 and 1856–58), and above all the Sino-Japanese War (1894–95), in which China's impotence and the failure of its 'self-strengthening' policy became dramatically evident, the Dowager Empress Cixi (regent for the minor Guangxi) was unable to deal with the country's financial problems and consequently became more and more indebted to the Western powers. The latter, in exchange for their loans, demanded greater privileges in the Chinese territory in an attempt to 'split it up'. The ruling class found itself faced with a drastic alternative: either take refuge in the traditional autarchy or make use of the bitter lesson and accept the fact that the measures undertaken until then to reform and modernise the millenary Chinese reality had been thoroughly inadequate. The failure of the reforms forced the Empress to seek a way to direct the growing discontent away from the throne and towards the foreigners in particular and their properties. This xenophobic attitude intensified especially among the reactionary clique of the court led by the Manchu Prince Duan. It was in this climate that the extremist xenophobic sect of the Fists of Right and Harmony continued to flourish (*Yihe quan*, known in the West as the Boxers). The expansion of the great colonial empires within the country provoked the violent opposition of the Chinese masses, who had been struck by the collapse of the peasant artisan economy and natural disasters. This opposition was directed by secret societies linked to the rural area and was aimed primarily against the missions and Chinese Christians.

In 1905, some Chinese students in Japan founded a nationalist association under the direction of Sun Yat-sen that was later formalised with the creation of the Guomindang (Nationalist Party) and supported by Chinese residents abroad. In 1911, a series of revolts for secession broke out at Wuchang (the present Wuhan) and spread to the rest of the country, forcing the court to flee from the Forbidden City and Peking. The chief instigators were the men of the New Army who some time before had begun to turn against the Manchus. On 12 February 1912, the last Qing emperor, Puyi, was forced to abdicate and two days later General Yuan Shikai became the first president of the Republic.

That which is usually called the "Revolution of 1911" was nothing but a moment of transition, a compromise: in fact, it was directed against the Manchu domination, thereby concealing the internal social conflicts. (*c.b.*)

Bibliography
M. Sabattini and P. Santangelo, *Storia della Cina*. Rome: Laterza, 1986.
H. Frank and R. Trauzettel, *Das chinesische Kaiserreich*. Frankfurt am Main and Hamburg: Fischer Bücherei, 1967.
M. Bastid, M. C. Bergére and J. Chesneaux, *China from the Opium Wars to the 1911 Revolution*. Hassocks: Harvester Press, 1977.

23.
Guards at the town gate at Hanzhong
with the mortars, Imperial period.

24.
*A corner of the crenellated wall with a small
fort at Hanzhong.*

25.
View of Hanzhong across a canal.
The elegant residence of a Mandarin can
be seen on the right.

26.
River outside the main gate of a walled city.

*'Military drills a few days before
the Revolution' (Nani's caption).*

Between the Empire and the Republic

29.
Prisoners being transported in narrow
wooden cages are observed by the curious.

30.
Procession of an official with his escort, signs and gong, crossing the Han river. The official is on a sedan chair.

31.
Public execution of a man sentenced to death by strangling. The by now lifeless man is still tied to the post.

32.
Residence of the Mandarin of the Chenggu Xian district. The two cages at the sides of the entrance gate were used for a slow and cruel capital punishment. A prisoner chained to a large stone is on the left.

35.
A Mandarin seated in the centre of his numerous escort. Indicated on the chest of each soldier is his rank and province of origin. The two large characters on the last two soldiers on the right (as on others) mean 'bodyguard'.

36.
A Mandarin in the centre, surrounded by his personal escort, armed with rifles and bandoliers filled with cartridges.

37.
'Republican soldiers at Hanzhong in 1914'
(Nani's caption).

38.
Soldiers in Western uniforms.

A Republican Army division lines up for a military parade at Hanzhong. The contrast of the new uniforms with those of the Imperial period is evident.

The People

During his stay in China, Father Leone Nani made an extraordinary series of portraits. These show his great interest and sensitivity for the people he met and immortalised in different poses and situations, and leave behind a kind of 'catalogue' of the human types in China in the early twentieth century. Just like any other portrait photographer of the time, Nani also paid particular attention to the settings, using a series of props to decorate his photography 'set' from time to time. The same backgrounds frequently appear, at times they are neutral, but more often rather elaborate; there are European clocks, the symbol of a certain well-being, but also spittoons, globes, inlaid chairs, teacups and water-pipes. Sometimes the men hold a cigar or cigarette between their fingers, while the women often flaunt a pendant watch at the fastening of their gown. These portraits were executed according to very precise aesthetic canons which were in use those days, and according to a rigidly defined formal plan, that of the *carte de visite*. The light is soft and diffused, the gaze fixed on the camera, the pose static, the faces impassive or barely smiling.

The many similarities linking these portraits lead one to think that his style of work was systematic, cold and serial. After a more attentive observation, however, not only the missionary-photographer's curiosity and attention to the composition emerge, but also a desire to reflect the physiognomies and costumes that create a variegated mosaic of personalities and reveal his profound anthropological interest. The details are fundamental: the use of Western hats on the part of some young Chinese, the safety pin closing the collar of an impassive official, the resigned look on a young woman's face or the crossed legs of a bridal couple, all of which become emblems of intimacy. These elements bear witness to Nani's acute capacity of observation as well as his creative vein. But they also speak of his wish to document and inform about a world—and above all about its people—that was still so distant and unknown to the Italian public. For this reason, he also produced some real reportages, texts complete with photos, some of which unfortunately have been lost. The many photos that do remain, however, document everyday existence as they catch people in particular moments of their lives.

40.
A young woman in a 'modern' costume:
a long skirt and a watch on her chest.

41.
Portrait of a well-off man in an exquisitely
Chinese interior, emphasised by the peony-
decorated vase and the three wall scrolls.

42.
Peasant family around a table in front of their thatch-roofed, mud house.

43.
Dinner out-of-doors.

44.
Group of women and children of a modest social condition: the women wear their everyday clothes and two children on the left are barefoot.

45.
A peasant couple travelling. The man wears braided straw sandals on his feet, the footwear of the poor.

46.
*Group of mothers, probably in front of
a church. Their head-dress identifies them
as Christians.*

47.
Wife and concubines of an Imperial
government dignitary. The little boy wears
an amulet against evil spirits on his jacket.

48.
Three generations of women portrayed
together: the little girl is dressed up for
an important occasion, her mother and
grandmother are on either side. To be noted
in this photo, as in others, the women's
bound feet in their tiny shoes.

49.
Group of people gathered together in a typical reception room.

50.
Group portrait of two men and two children. Of interest is the little boy who reads, or pretends to do so.

51.
An elderly couple. The rigid pose of the two, sitting with their hands on their laps, is intentionally static.

52.
A military Mandarin of the fourth grade with his wife and children. The embroidered tiger design on his chest and the opaque blue 'button' of his head-dress are signs of his rank.

53.
A man with his beast of burden laden with goods and animals. In the mountain Vicariate of Hanzhong there were no carriage roads: goods were transported on one's back or on beasts of burden since carts could not be used.

54.
A man of an elevated social condition posing in front of the camera wearing his best clothes and holding a water-pipe. Next to him is a globe—an object, like the clock, that often appears in Father Nani's photographs.

55.
A mother and her child. As in other photos of Nani, attention has been paid to background details.

56.
Portrait of a woman of high rank.

57.
Portrait of a young bridal couple.
The attempt here is at a less static pose:
the two are portrayed standing and
holding hands, with the man holding
a Western-style hat and the bride
a handkerchief.

58.
A grandfather posing with his grandson.
Their simple clothes and the wooden chair
indicate a modest social standing.

59.
Man holding a sword, probably a small landowner of the region, flanked by two helpers.

60.
Two prosperous citizens have their portrait taken in the inside courtyard at the main house of the Hanzhong mission. They wear a 'hat' called guapimao *(a 'watermelon skin cap', referring of course to its shape).*

61.
One of the leading citizens holding a water pipe. On the table to his right an accumulation of items make up the scene; among them a clock imported from the West, an object much loved by the Chinese.

62.
Portrait of a man, without backdrop; but we see the inevitable stand with the usual array of scenographic objects.

The People

63.
*Soldiers of the new Republican Army in
Western-style uniforms in front of a barrack.*

64.
*An officer of the new Republican Army poses
stiffly in his uniform, an imposing sword
in his hand and… a safety pin closing
his collar.*

65.
Two young students waiting to take the State exam to become officers posing with fans and Western-type umbrellas in their hands.

66.
Lotus in flower. The root, or rather the 'rhizome of the lotus' (in Chinese, genjing*), is edible.*

Life and Work

The waters

The three great rivers of northern China (Luo He, Huang He and Wei He) symbolise the first three dynasties. According to legend, the mythical emperor Yu, founder of the Xia dynasty (twenty-second – sixteenth centuries BC circa) subdued the waters and dominated the rivers. It was under the Western Zhou (eleventh century circa – 770 BC) that the valley of the Yellow River (Huang He) was controlled by means of a system of signal towers that could warn of an eventual barbarian invasion as well as, and above all, control the hydro-geological condition of the region, that is the danger of swollen rivers and floods, a recurring threat in the history of China from ancient times. Therefore, the fortune and/or misfortune of the ruling class depended on the relationship between state power and the control of the waters. It is not surprising that the Chinese symbol for the Yellow River is the both beneficial and malefic dragon, a symbol present in all of popular traditions. And every river has its own tutelary god who is venerated; in ancient times human sacrifices were offered, which were later substituted by ritual ones in the temples.

The fact that Chinese bureaucratic society needed great works of irrigation and conservation made hydraulic engineering a highly esteemed activity among the state officials; it contributed, moreover, to stabilising and supporting the type of society in which such works were an essential part. It is worth mentioning here the construction of the Grand Canal, the most ancient mountain canal ever achieved by any civilisation: it links northern China with the south, Peking and Hangzhou to be precise, for 2,500 kilometres over a ten-degree span of latitude.

Typical of northern China are the terraced fields of cultivation, irrigated by means of a complicated system of canalisation of the waters. The watermill made its first appearance during the Wang Mang era (9–23 AD, the period of interregnum between the dynasties of the Eastern and Western Han): it consisted of a battery of pylons alimented by a horizontal camshaft and operated by a vertically placed wheel in a stream of water. The hydro-graphical system also served as a means of communication for peasant communities that were spread out over the vast territory, providing for the distribution and exchange of goods, as well as for the transport of grain collected for tribute payments.

Cormorant fishing was practised along the water courses: with a wire round its neck and a cord tied to one foot so that it could not fly away, the bird regurgitated into the boats the live fish it had caught but not swallowed. This ancient practice still continues today, but exclusively as a tourist attraction on the Li river at Guilin in southern China.

Agriculture

In China there are two principal fertile areas, each around one of the bigger rivers: the Yellow River (Huang He) in the north and the Long River (Chang Jiang or Yangtze) in the south. In the northern zone there are fertile lands of loess, formed by sandy clay deposits that come from the Gobi desert: with good fertilisation these lands can be exploited with intensive cultivation of wheat, millet, barley, beans and hemp. In the southern zone, rice is the chief crop in the winter, and when the rice paddies have dried, then wheat, beans, turnips or barley are grown.

In order to deal with the problem of sufficient food supplies, the Chinese had already introduced during the Han era much more intensive farming than anywhere else in the West. The need for additional farmland led the rulers in the Song era (960–1279) to recur to terracing and other forms of land reclamation: some lakes were drained and transformed into cultivatable fields that were protected from the waters by earthen dykes and bamboo rafts covered with aquatic grasses and earth.

Up until the Tang era (618–907), the Chinese invented a variety of farm tools that were suitable for the type of farming they practised. They possessed a mechanical sower and a series of harrows and rollers, and they fixed hoes to a frame that could be dragged through the rows of plants. However, it was not until the thirteen century that a great innovation appeared: this was a rotating sifting machine that remained unknown in Europe until the eighteenth century.

Botanical studies flourished in China as early as the third century BC, and treatises of botany and plant therapy were compiled throughout the different dynasties. State bureaucracy attributed particular importance to the correct use of the land, and encouraged the development of geo-botany so as to know more about plants and the different environments in which they grew.

Paper

China's contribution to the development of science and technology has been noteworthy and was underestimated by our scholars for many centuries. And yet it was China long before the West that came up with such inventions as the techniques for working iron and bronze, mechanical clocks, the driving belt, moveable type, gunpowder, the stern rudder-post, the seismograph, windmills and many others.

Among the things they invented was paper. In the *Dynastic History of the Former Han*, Fan Ye, who lived in the fifth century, wrote the biography of Cai Lun in which is written: 'In ancient times books were made with bamboo strips or pieces of silk. But the first were voluminous and the second costly. Cai Lun then suggested that bark, hemp, rags and old fishnets be used to make paper. In 105 BC he presented his invention to the Emperor He of the Eastern Han who praised him for his cleverness. Since then paper has been greatly used'. Other historical documents say that paper had already been in use before 105. Xu Sheng, a contemporary of Cai Lun, in his *Analytical Dictionary of Characters*, completed in the year 100, had described the process of papermaking, which was then done by macerating scraps of silk in water; the liquid was then poured over bamboo screens and left to dry. Cai Lun has been credited with having perfected and developed the technique of papermaking by using other elements; that method then spread outside of the country during the Tang dynasty (618–907), the period of greatest political and territorial expansion.

It is curious to observe how the ideogram expressing 'character' in Chinese is composed of the graph for 'roof' under which is placed the one for 'baby'. This ancient pictogram of semantic valence indicates that a 'character' must be looked after with love and care just like a baby in the house, because it was written on perishable materials like bamboo strips or silk. Starting in 221 BC, that is, from the time the Emperor Shihuang of the Qin dynasty established the Empire and standardised the graphic norms, the written language became a contributing factor to the unity of Chinese culture, notwithstanding the great geographical barriers that divided the scenario of its development.

Silk

While there was already mention of the raising of silkworms during the Zhou dynasty (eleventh century BC), fragments of that precious cloth seem to date back to 1500 BC. According to legend, it was the consort of the mythical Yellow Emperor who had the idea of weaving those valuable threads, which were then being used as strings for musical instruments, in order to make precious cloths.

When silk reached Rome some time during the first century, it was called *sericum* in Latin, that is, *ser* cloth (probably an approximate and distorted phonetic of the Chinese word for silk which is *si*, where the 'i' is mute), and for the ancient Romans its value was equal to that of gold.

Exported silk was either woven or in hanks, for it was forbidden to reveal the secret of silkworm production or send cocoons out of the country. But legend has it that in the fifth century AD, a Chinese princess who had married the King of Khotan—one of the oasis kingdoms along the Silk Road—had hidden some eggs in her head-dress. It seems that the two monks who reached Justinian's court around 550 announcing that they came from the land of Seres and knew how silk was produced were from Khotan and not from China.

In ancient times only members of the imperial family and of the court were allowed to wear silk: yellow was the colour destined for the emperor, his first wife and his heir; the other wives wore purple silk as did high-ranking officials, while those of lower rank dressed in red silk.

Medicine

Ancient Chinese medicine was closely tied to Taoism and the shamanism of North Asian tribal healers and magicians. During the era of Confucius doctors could already be distinguished from itinerant empirics, and during the subsequent eras some scholars embraced the medical profession thus turning it into a prestigious profession.

Traditional medicine based diagnosis on a prolonged and attentive examination of the pulse: the human body was compared to a stringed instrument, and the harmonies and dissonances of the organism could only be ascertained by feeling the pulse, wherein flowed the vital elements. The prevention of disease was considered much more important than controlling it when it appeared, and in spite of the recourse to charms and exorcisms, particularly among the poorer classes of society, Chinese medicine was thoroughly rational. The existence of an administration, which only educated people who had passed qualifying exams could accede to, later favoured the extension of analogous exams for those scientific activities, among which medicine, that were considered essential to the State. During the Tang period, around the seventh century, the first imperial medical school was established.

There are numerous statuettes in precious and less precious materials, most often in jade or ivory, representing nude women lying on a bed and touching different parts of their bodies with their hands. Women used these statuettes to indicate the painful parts or zones of their bodies to the doctor, since they could not undress in front of him.

Gunpowder

The invention of gunpowder was probably accidental: indeed, the research of the Taoist alchemists investigated the properties of different substances in an attempt to found the elixir of life or the drug of immortality. One of these substances, saltpetre (potassium nitrate) was used to dissolve metals, but when mixed with charcoal and sulphur provoked a deflagration. These three substances were used separately in traditional Chinese medicine. Invented between the seventh and ninth centuries, but not for bellicose use, gunpowder was employed only around 1000 for the construction of explosive weapons. A manual of military techniques dated 1044 contains the first formulas for the composition of gunpowder for different types of firearms. The *pilipao* (thundering catapults) used by the Song to defend themselves from the Jin Tartars were the precursors of cannon and rifles: they were made of bamboo tubes that propelled rockets. (*c.b.*)

Bibliography

E. Balazs, *Chinese Civilization and Bureaucracy, Variations on a Theme*. New Haven: Yale University Press, 1964.

J. Needham, *Scienza e civiltà in Cina*. Turin: Einaudi Editore, 1981, vol. 1, *Lineamenti introduttivi*.

J. Gernet, *Le monde chinois*. Paris: A. Colin, 1972.

E. Collotti Pischel, *Cultura Cinese: Storia*. Milan: Libreria Universitaria CUESP, 2002.

W. Eberhard, *A Dictionary of Chinese Symbols*. London and New York: Routledge & Kegan Paul, 1986.

Liu Guojun and Zheng Rusi, *The Story of Chinese Books*. Beijing: Foreign Languages Press, 1985.

A. Forte, 'Scienza e tecnica', in *Cina a Venezia*. Milan: Electa, 1986.

Ancient China's Technology and Science, compiled by the Institute of the History of Natural Sciences, Chinese Academy of Sciences, Foreign Languages Press. Beijing, 1983.

Un miliardo di uomini: Cina, il passato e il presente. Milan: Arnoldo Mondadori, 1980.

P. Huard and Ming Wong, *La medicina cinese*. Milan: Il Saggiatore, 1967.

67.
Boats, nets and cormorants used for fishing on the Han river. These big aquatic birds were raised and tamed to capture fish in their beaks and bring them back to their masters.

68.
Fisherman looking after cormorants.

69.
Cormorant fishing.

72.
Rowers on the Han river.

73.
The positioning of weighted baskets to divert the river water or reinforce the banks.

74.
Men and boys consolidating the riverbanks
in order to control the frequent floods
of the Han river.

75.
*Construction work on a bridge over
the Han river.*

76.
An affluent of the Han river enroute to Huayang. The movement of the swollen, rapidly moving waters was photographed by Father Nani with remarkable ability, notwithstanding the rudimentary technical means at his disposal.

77.
*The dangerous rapids of the 'Golden Gorge'
in the Han river, also known as the 'tortoise
rapids' because of a large rock that rises
in the middle of the river and looks like
an enormous tortoise shell.*

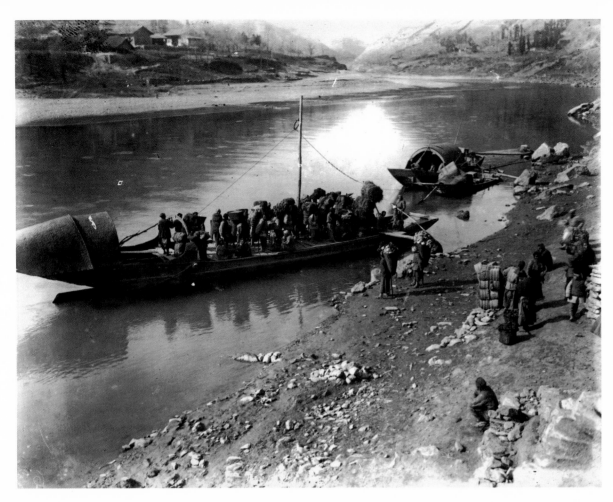

78.
A cargo of goods on a junk along the Han river, an important means of communication and transport in the south of Shaanxi province.

79.
Fishermen with cormorants along the riverbanks.

80.
*The solitary boat with unfurled sails seems
lost on the great river.*

81.
A bamboo wheel, driven by the current of the Han river, carries water to the irrigation canals.

82.
Terraced wheat fields.

83.
Hills in the mist. Father Nani obviously wants his photograph to reproduce a favourite subject of Chinese painting; we notice the retouching after the picture was taken.

84.
Scenes of life: the grinding of wheat.

85.
Scenes of daily life in a mountain village.
Mules, waiting to be laden with goods for
transport, wait beside straw-roofed houses.

86.
A procession along a recently mown field.

Life and Work

90.
Peasants taking a rest from their work
in the fields.

94.
*Children grinding soybeans, a legume that is widespread in China and also used to make a kind of cheese (*doufu*).*

95.
*The interior of a paper mill. The sheets of
paper are pressed to eliminate the water that
accumulated during their manufacture.*

96.
*Papermaking: cistern for the preparation
of the bamboo-wood mixture.*

97.
Some miners pulling their loads from the underground passage of a coal mine.

Life and Work

98.
Gold diggers.

99.
Gold diggers 'cleaning' a large sieve.

Life and Work

101.
Wood vendors in a village.

102.
Workers lacquering furniture.

103.
Two woodcutters chopping down a big tree trunk with their hatchets.

104.
The casting of a bell. The metal was poured into an underground mould.

105.
Men at a well.

106.
Grinding gunpowder.

107.
*A travelling barber 'delicately' delouses
a client's head.*

108.
Silk weaving. The precious thread is unravelled from cocoons immersed in hot water, and is then wound onto a skein-winder that is operated by a pedal.

109.
The production of mats from vegetable fibres.

110.
*A group of hunters pose proudly in front
of the wild boar they have just killed.*

Life and Work

111.
Hunter with a fuse-operated rifle. The barrel is so long that he needs a helper.

112.
A doctor feeling a patient's pulse in order to diagnose her illness. This was the only kind of physical contact permitted with women.

113.
A man bending wood that will be used to make bows.

114.
Rope maker on the Han river.

115.
Spinning cotton outdoors. In southern Shaanxi, this plant grows so abundantly that it is harvested twice a year.

116.
Shoemaker or better, 'slipper maker'.
This type of footwear is still used by Chinese
peasants.

117.
*The village blacksmith working
in his rudimentary smithy.*

118.
An embalmer at work on a splendid example of leopard captured in the Qin Ling mountains.

119.
Mountain bearers, carrying perfectly balanced loads on their backs, arriving in town.

120.
An elderly gunsmith, assisted by his two sons, building a rifle barrel, using a crank handle drill.

121.
A workshop making straw sandals.

122.
Craftsman working at a turning-lathe.

123.
Peasants weighing a piglet.

Places of the Spirit

Religion and Art

The world of China knows nothing of the concept of 'religion' in the Western sense. They might speak of 'schools' or 'doctrines', but there has never been anything approaching a clearly defined religion. Consequently the concepts of State Religion, clergy or wars of religion are absolutely foreign to the Chinese mentality.

We can identify two great schools of thought in the fields of philosophic and religious experience: Confucianism and the Tao. Confucianism—a doctrine which has always provided a basis for morality among the peoples of the Far East—arose from the first local cults of peasant civilisation, the traditions of seasonal festivals, the habits and customs of farming communities and fortified villages. The Doctrine of Confucius, as collected in the *Dialogues* and the *Analects* contains the entire list of rules for social behaviour and has contributed to the backbone of the Imperial system for more than two thousand years. Taoism derives from beliefs connected to the changes in climate, the progress of time and seasons and is directly related to the world of nature. As opposed to the rigid Confucian norms of etiquette and ceremonial, Taoist thought inclines to 'non-action' (*wuwei*) and 'long life' (*changshou*).

Both Lao-ze and Confucius—they both probably lived between the sixth and fifth centuries BC—left an immense heritage of wisdom which was to be developed and enriched by various thinkers in the epoch that followed, a period of great intellectual ferment known as the 'Hundred Schools' (Bai jia). Buddhism entered China as a 'foreign' religion following the fall of the Later Han dynasty (around the third–fourth century AD). It mostly arrived from the dusty caravan routes of central Asia, together with the central-Asiatic dynasties installed on the edge of the Mongolian steppes.

Buddhism came as an ecumenical religion of salvation, but in no way contrasted existing religious beliefs. It was based on faith in *kharma* and palingenesis. Every life was subject the ineluctable law of cause and effect: all good and evil actions met their reward or punishment in a future life. The doctrine of Buddha pointed the way to a definitive liberation from the cycle of rebirth, hence the way to illumination and *nirvana* which lies beyond all earthly and heavenly kingdoms.

So, we can speak of 'three religions' (*san jiao*)—but also of many forms of religious syncretism—that with alternating periods of ascendancy, have co-existed throughout the entire history of China. Ancestor worship—originally linked to the cults of the seasons, whereas much later it assumed the aspect of a purely domestic cult—was practised to show respect and devotion, and to ingratiate the benevolence of the ancestors, since it was believed that the spirits of the dead influenced the lives of their descendants on earth.

This ties in with the Confucian concept of 'filial piety', where the younger generations are debtors to the older, and are bound to look after them, not only in this life but also in the life to come. In their homes we find altars dedicated to the ancestors, upon which 'funerary tablets' are placed; an essential feature of domestic architecture: rich families have rooms or temples set aside and furnished for praying.

In the countryside most of the houses have only one room. In the south-west corner, the darkest where the seed is stored stands the matrimonial bed where women give birth to new life. In ancient times the dead were also buried in this dark corner. This gave rise to the belief that it was exactly here, where the ancestors had left their mortal bodies, that the principles of life fluctuated, so that every birth seemed to be the reincarnation of an ancestor. This was the origin of the practice of geomancy (*Feng Shui*, literally "Wind and Water'), according to which the environment and its latent forces shed their influence on life and on the well-being of man. Nobody built a house or chose a burial plot or set a date to their marriage without consulting a geomancer.

Until 1949 a marriage was never decided by the couple concerned. It was a 'political' union between two families proposed by a marriage broker. In ancient China the young men were brought to the villages of their *fiancées* in the rest periods from their work in the fields (significant of a system that was originally matriarchal is the fact that the word *xing*, the Chinese for 'surname' still retains the key—or radical—of 'woman' to this day; while in sources that have come down to us, it was the girls who were exchanged. The most pathetic lament of many ancient ballads is that of the brides who were forced to go and live in 'foreign' villages. They were brought there in a hand-carried litter, accompanied by musicians whose role was to announce the marriage, and also to play music loud enough to drown the wailing of the brides. The colour of weddings is red, the good omen symbol is the red character of 'double happiness', as opposed to white which is associated with the west, the colour of autumn, old age and, by semantic extension, mourning. A man could marry one woman only, but was allowed to take one or more concubines.

Music and Opera

The first evidence of musical instruments goes back to the Shang dynasty (seventeenth to eleventh centuries BC) as revealed by archaeological discoveries. These were used in divinatory ceremonies presided over by the Emperor who was known as 'the First Magician of the Realm'. The first writings on music were reported in the *Ligi* ('Memories of Rituals') attributed to disciples of Confucius.

In ancient China music was considered an art for improving the manners and education of young people, but it also carried metaphysical meanings: in ceremonies ('rituals' according to the Confucian concept) a perfect performance contributed to maintaining the equilibrium between Heaven and Earth, and hence the stability of the Empire. Magical powers attributed to sounds explain some peculiarities of traditional Chinese music, such as its slowness and its emphasis on the materiality of each sound as a source of meditation.

By the last century BC 24 different instruments had developed and, through the centuries, five distinct categories of music: song, dance music, music for accompaniment, stage music and instrumental music.

Traditional instruments were subdivided into: stringed (like the *hugin*, a two-string violin); plucked (like the *pipa*, the most popular and best known among the lute family); wind (like the flute, *di*, which was a length of bamboo with 8 holes); percussion (a number of little bells in wood or metal, cymbals, various types of drums and, most famous of all, the *gong*).

Opera is the principal dramatic art and covers a wide variety of techniques for performance, such as singing, music, declamation and stylised combats, all accompanied by instrumental music. Over three hundred types of traditional operas are known. The main ones are: Peking Opera (Jingju), Hebei Opera (Pingju), Shaoxing Opera, Henan Opera (Yuju), Guandong Opera (Yueju) and Sichuan Opera (Chuanju).

The most ancient theatrical text known to us goes back to the thirteenth century AD, a period when China was ruled by a foreign dynasty, the Mongols, who assumed the name of the Chinese dynasty Yuan (1272–1368). The state 'nomenklatura' (held until then by officials who were also men of letters recruited under a system of imperial examinations based on knowledge of Confucian classics) found themselves 'out of a job' after the abolition of the exams. It was then that these men of letters, who had always harboured lofty prejudices against popular expressions of art, devoted themselves to writing for the theatre, which was the one entertainment their barbaric overlords passionately adored. Even during the previous Song dynasty (960–1279) the town markets were frequented by story-tellers, musicians, dancers, acrobats (types of popular art strictly connected with the daily life and religious sacrificial rituals), clowns and singers, who delighted both nobles and populace with their performances without actually attaining the rank of artists.

The actors—always men, even in the female roles—wore costumes with their faces painted to represent the various social castes. Over the centuries over five hundred different types of face make-up developed: for example, gold and silver symbolised nobility and saintliness as was used for Buddhist characters or gods; white was for traitors; red for the bold heroes. (*c.b.*)

Bibliography
W. Willetts, *Foundations of Chinese Art from Neolithic Pottery to Modern Architecture*. New York: McGraw-Hill, 1965.

M. Granet, *The Religion of the Chinese People*. New York: Harper & Row, 1975.

W. Eberhard, *A Dictionary of Chinese Symbols*. London and New York: Routledge & Kegan Paul, 1986.

T. C. Lai and R. Mok, *Jade flute: The Story of Chinese Music*. Hong Kong: Hong Kong Book Center, 1981.

L. Lanciotti, *Letteratura cinese*. Milan: Casa Editrice Dr. F. Vallardi, 1969.

A. Lavagnino, *Cultura cinese 1*. Milan: Libreria universitaria Cuesp, 2002.

R. Pisu and H. Tomiyama, *L'opera di Pechino*. Milan: Arnoldo Mondadori Editore, 1982.

Wu Weijie, *Tradizione e realtà del teatro cinese*. Milan: International Cultural Exchange, 1995.

126.
Ruins of a pagoda near Hanzhong.

127.
'Stone memorial tablets commemorating famous Mandarins' (Nani's caption).

128.
Weien Kukg Miao pagoda.

129.
Temple garden with many pavilions. We notice the bell and the drum which beat out the rhythm of life. In the foreground, the traditional incense burner.

130.
Small pagoda with lotus flower symbol.

131.
The Wanshou pagoda in Mian Xian,
in the prefecture of Hanzhong.

132.
The Yang-Hsien tower.

133.
Detail of a panel covered with ceramic tiles,
erected at the gate of a Taoist temple in
Yangxian.

134.
*Altar with the three Buddhas of the Past,
Present and Future.*

Places of the Spirit

135.
Representation of the tortures of hell in a Taoist temple.

136.
Interior of a temple with ex-votos.

137.
Ritual of suffrage for the deceased performed
before tablets of the ancestors displayed
for the ceremony.

138.
Suffrage ritual for the deceased.

139.
Funeral procession according to traditional Chinese rites. The inscriptions on the banners are eulogies of the deceased.

140.
Crowd waiting for the celebration of
a funeral. The coffin stands in the tent (left)
where rites and prayers are in progress.

141.
Funeral ceremony. Members of the family
offer incense and kneel before the altar.

142.
Funeral: hired assistants, with their heads covered by white cloths as a sign of mourning, prepare the fire-crackers to be let off during the funeral to drive away evil spirits.

143.
Funeral procession.

144.
Statues and objects in papier mâché *and wood, representing people and objects dear to the deceased, ready for burning so that he can enjoy them in the hereafter.*

145.
Geomancers at work to select a propitious place.

146.
*A company of strolling actors in the typical
costumes of classic opera.*

147.
A company of actors.

148.
Masks and costumes of traditional theatre.

Places of the Spirit

149.
*In musical drama women's roles are played
by men, who even wear special shoes to
imitate the 'gilded lotuses' of the women.*

150.
*Orchestra of the musical theatre: on the left,
player of the* huquin *(a type of violin),
beside him, player of the* pipa *(a guitar-like
instrument).*

151.
*A woman tightrope-walker performing
before a crowd of spectators.*

The Mission

The gospel message arrived in Xi'an, capital of the Shaanxi, in the time of the glorious Tang dynasty. It was here that the Emperor Gaozhong (628–83) officially recognised Christianity, brought to China by Syrian monks, as is testified by the Nestorian stele inscribed in 781, and preserved in the provincial museum of Xi'an. It is the most ancient monument documenting the presence of Christianity in China. The inscription, which was re-discovered in 1625, aroused great curiosity among the local men of letters, because together with the Chinese characters, the texts were inscribed in Syrian which was no longer understood. As a result, two officials of the Imperial Court in Peking, who had become Christians, asked the Jesuits to send them to a missionary who could study this important archaeological find. Not long after, Father Stefano Le Fèvre arrived and established himself in Hanzhong, a small remote town in the southern part of the province of Shaanxi, which can boast a long and consolidated presence of the Catholic Church. Ever since that time the Church has been established without interruption, and its communities have succeeded in surviving long and blood-thirsty persecutions. For two centuries the Franciscans were at work here, joined in 1885 by missionaries from the Roman Seminary for Foreign Missions, who in 1900 were forced to weather the cyclone of the Boxer Rebellion that brought about the death of some thirty thousand Christians. Among them was Father Alberto Crescitelli, barbarously slain on 21 July 1900 in the village of Yentsepien. He died at the age of 37, after 12 years missionary work in China. His copious correspondence, covering a host of topics, documents his interest in the culture, traditions and customs of the people of China. His style is characteristic of the work of that small group of Italian missionaries. It provided a clear example and inspiration for Father Leone Nani, who was to arrive in the region only a few years later.

The Apostolic Vicariate of southern Shaanxi, guided by a handful of missionaries from the Roman Seminary, covered an area of more than 80 square kilometres. The main towns were the two administrative centres of the prefectures: Hanzhong (which became the name of the Vicariate in the 1920s) and Xing-an, with 21 smaller towns and countless villages. When Father Nani arrived in a population of five million inhabitants, the converts exceeded 11 thousand and there were 1800 catechumens.

The principal residence of the mission was at Guluba. It was built in perfect Chinese style by the first Vicar Apostolic, Monsignor Gregorio Antonucci, who immediately went about founding a seminary as well as the orphanage placed in the care of Canossian nuns.

The first decade of the twentieth century was a time of great political upheaval in China. In the Shaanxi province, as in many other parts of the country, there were violent clashes between the upholders of the decadent Empire and the supporters of the new Republican party. The city of Hanzhong held out against the 'republicans' until the beginning of 1912.

Meanwhile the atmosphere towards foreigners and Christians was radically changing. The historian of the mission, Kenneth S. Latourette, could write that the years between 1901 and the outbreak of the First World War were the most fruitful for the Christian missions in China.

In 1914, when Father Nani was obliged to return to Italy, he left behind in his beloved mission in Hanzhong 14,000 Catholics distributed amongst 52 churches and chapels. Although, in the same year, the number of foreign priests in the mission had been reduced to 11, there was an increase, albeit modest, of Chinese priests, plus 4 clerics major and 16 seminarians. The local Church was beginning to strike solid roots.

152.
*The Cathedral dedicated
to Saints Peter and Paul, Guluba.*

153.
Father Scalzi at the Shishian (or Si-Hsiang)
residence.

154.
*Orphans found and educated by
the Canossian nuns before the church
at Guluba.*

155.
A group of orphans sewing at the orphanage for girls in Hanzhong.

156.
A group of boys performing gymnastics at a mission school.

157.
*'Mission church at Liukiain with
Father Ruggero Perotti on the right'
(Nani's caption).*

158.
*A group of Christians before
a small village church.*

The Mission

161.
Festoons and triumphal arches in
Hanzhong for the blessing of the Michael's
Cathedral (1913) and for the
25th anniversary of Monsignor Passerini's
ordination.

162.
*Monsignor Pio Giuseppe Passerini, Fathers
and notables (eminent citizens and
Mandarins) at St Michael's Cathedral in
Hanzhong on the occasion of the blessing of
the cathedral (11 December 1913) and the
25th anniversary of his priesthood (he was
ordained on 22 December 1888).
Father Nani stands in the top row, second
to the right of the column.*

163.
Monsignor Passerini with missionaries and local personalities. Father Nani stands in the centre behind the apostolic administrator.

164.
At the centre of the bottom row: Monsignor Passerini, to his right Father Enrico Scalzi; to his left, Father Giocchino Piazzalunga. Father Nani stands at top right.

Writings

In Father Nani's day precise rules for a standard transliteration of the Chinese characters did not exist; hence Nani's considerable freedom in the spelling of Chinese names and terms, a usual practice early in the last century. Thus Nani writes Hanchungfu, Hanchunfu or Hanchung for the name of the town we would now call Hanzhong; Shen-si or Shensi for Shaanxi, Culupa for Guluba, Szechuan or Szechwan instead of Sichuan, while his Sianfu is today written Xi'an. All Nani's texts, of which the following are a selection, can be found in the PIME General Archive in Rome, title XXIII, volume 10.

Newsletters

The Abolition of Opium

In recent times when a certain trend towards progress can be now be discerned, the cohort of nobles of the Dragon Empire has more or less come to the conclusion that one of the encroaching causes of the centuries-old moral and material decadence of their infinite people is the extraordinary abuse of opium.

Right up to the present day generation after generation have been inebriating themselves without the least restraint around the poisonous 'cannuccia' (the pipe), voraciously absorbing the hypnotic and narcotic smoke with a languid eye, as they poison their blood, and sully and drug their mental and moral faculties, precociously subjecting them to an invincible and incurable craze for this slow, sleepy poison.

In every epoch down to the present the history of opium in the Celestial Empire has revealed horrifying pages of facts, and things that are both public and within the family circles; from the imperial palace to the hovel of the lowliest beggar. But none of this could halt for a single moment the hypnotic torrent that sweeps on to overwhelm and fatally corrupt a people, an entire nation…

Europeans in China have witnessed these terrible effects. These devastating conclusions, shared alike by the most progressive Chinese dignitaries and the foreign nations, gave rise to the humanitarian idea of putting a stop to it, decreeing the complete abolition of the poppy (*papaver sonniferum*) and consequently of the immense masses of opium smokers. However the first imperial decrees proclaimed in every district were so incomprehensible, or worded so vaguely, that the people made fun of them or else interpreted them to their own advantage.

On the one hand the magistrates who did not want to be bound by the new orders, or secretly smoked opium themselves, were removed from office; on the other hand prizes and promotion were awarded to the cultivated Mandarins and men of letters who supported and championed the early stages of the anti-opium campaign.

In every province however it was necessary to introduce pharmaceuticals in the form of powders, syrups and pills, almost all of them with a morphine base to effect a gradual cure, in order to allay the so-called 'craze', until there was a overall chance of eradicating this poisonous abuse.

After some time had elapsed, clearer and more threatening edicts were issued and the authorities of every department (of course flattered by pipe-dream prospects of promotion, as well as those who might be open to denunciation themselves) were eagle-eyed in their surveillance of forbidden crops of poppies, since they were liable to confiscation of their land, as well as the heavy fines for undeclared opium dealers or recalcitrant smokers.

At the same time the guards at the opium toll stations (import tariffs apart) required a much closer surveillance: opium dealers were suppressed, except for a few official shops where only a certain amount of opium could be bought under a special, personally identified permit.

In the light of these improvements the anti-opium crusade advanced to the point where things gradually began to take on an air of seriousness.

Naturally the price of opium leaped to a level practically out of the reach of the middle classes; for most people it was obviously necessary to abandon a vice that cost so heavy a price.

The latest official instructions for this year spurred the Mandarins and delegates to activity. They were expressly sent out to every place where the poppies were beginning to sprout in abundance so that they were able to identify illegal crops with their own eyes.[1]

In view of the animosity that resulted from so much constant intrigue to attain their purposes, the usual reprisals, at times serious fighting on the part of the people, were only to be expected. Nor, to tell the truth, was the new situation lacking in opportunities for the Mandarins and their subordinates to satisfy their greed. At all events, we can almost assert that this present anti-opium crusade has roused China from its long and deep lethargy as it attempts to take its first steps towards physical and moral progress for the benefit of its immense population.

But this is to assume that the people themselves are sincerely convinced. If the crusade were to fail, then—woe to the Empire of dreams! Woe to the narcotic Empire!

Hanchungfu 1911 (sheet 1059)

[1] It is said that a passing delegate, unaware of the time the poppy came into flower, was hoodwinked by a Mandarin who took advantage of his ignorance, and reaped a high percentage on the opium crops when they were removed; at a sum agreed upon with the connivance of the interested parties.

The Last of the Pigtail

Once the infant 'middle flower' republic had dethroned the infamous Manchu dynasty, it needed to sweat blood to restore something approaching order and assure the masses a certain calm, since they were already pessimistic in regard to the future of their country.

In the meantime the new political world of China seems totally absorbed in carrying out grandiose projects for general reform, trusting to a new era of progress and civilisation, which includes the absolute expulsion of any trace of a Manchu aroma.

Of interest and curiosity in these days of 'Risorgimento' are the virtually harmless popular movements resulting from the war on 'pigtails', already foreseen as inevitable. Today, if a Chinese wants to be a patriot of his newly liberated homeland, he must above all rid himself of that ridiculous appendage of Manchu slavery, the pigtail.

The nobles and the new Chinese authorities have set a magnificent example, unlike the tillers of the soil, or the populace who live outside the towns, isolated from all political events. They are perplexed and disconcerted by the continual posting of official decrees proclaiming the inexorable shearing of the 'pigtail'. So it is hardly surprising to find that many of them are still resisting and fighting tooth and nail these proclamations and threats in order to avoid the disgrace inflicted on what has been for centuries of generations their dearest and most decorous adornment of personal beauty. Even worse, the cutting off of the pigtail and the shaving of a rich crop of hair would most likely produce an unfortunate resemblance to the Bonzes, which would make them a laughing stock. For a Chinaman pays far more attention to his outer appearance than is commonly supposed; almost to the point of superstition.

To soothe this discontent and remedy such surprising reluctance on the part of the people, soldiers of the garrison were stationed the gates of the town, and the commanding officers of the territorial guards of the villages take offenders into custody and cut off the pigtails of all those who have failed to do so. In some places they have gone so far as forcing the recalcitrant to either allow their pigtails to be cut off, or else pay a fine of 500 sapeks (about 1.50 lire). Not a few of the die-hards now find it easier to sacrifice themselves rather than do themselves so much financial harm.

Small shops and businesses have also suffered because many people did not dare to frequent the town or the markets with their cereals and grain to sell, or to purchase goods for their families, since they were afraid some vandal would make an attack on their pigtails. In fact it seemed much more heroic and wiser to stay locked in the house. Especially when news arrived that, in the town of Lan Chou in the neighbouring province of Kan-su, a revolt had broken out in June, a revolt against anyone who cut off pigtails.

By far the greater part of the population however who had republican convictions, to some degree, resigned themselves to getting rid of their greasy ornament, and arranged their hair in strange outlandish styles according to their taste, or else to express their regret.

Recently the barbers have also been given public warning to the effect that they will be forbidden from exercising an ignoble trade according to the ancient custom, on punishment of flogging and a fine as well… Under the newly eclipsed empire of 'pigtails', when litigants quarrelled and were about to come to blows they would first, according to custom, pull each other's pigtail. Thieves and rogues were captured by the 'tail', which was used to

tie them to a post or a tree, or even hung in the air by it while they were compelled to answer the charges against them.

Apart from these and similar cases, anyone wishing to show contempt would simply touch his pigtail, a serious insult. Moreover etiquette demanded that, when brought before the authorities or superiors, and in circumstances of solemn celebrations, pigtails were required to hang neatly down the back between the shoulders.

The Mandarins have now abandoned what used to be the customary uniform of Manchu ritual, and very soon will have the new uniform: the new 'seals of office' have already been distributed and it is hoped that the new civil and penal codes for the reforming republic will be ready by the end of the year.

Now that these sons of the 'flowering Republic' are losing their pigtails and dreaming up new laws and customs to which the whole population will have to submit, it is to be hoped that their minds, dulled as they have been by a poisonous narcotic and obstinate supine ignorance, will shake off this centuries-old torpor and open up to Christian civilisation. Thus they will experience that sublime and simple morality which alone can rightly educate the heart and ennoble the man, placing him in society as an effective instrument of progress and a support for his country.

Hanchungfu, July 1912 (sheet 1089)

The Italian Vicariate of Hanchung and how they Saved the Authorities from the Violence of the Revolution

More and more poor Manchu families move us to the utmost pity. They wander about in terror in search of some refuge or hiding place to escape the wild incursions of armed revolutionaries that have sworn to exterminate the entire race of Manchus from the face of China.

No door dares open to take these wretched people in because in so doing they would be exposed to the serious charge of complicity. Thus, all these fugitives can do is to run from one village to another and, only in the most desperate moments, abandon hope and die by their own hand, rather than submit to the mercies of the anarchist fury.

What can we say of all those men holding high and powerful positions, who now find themselves besieged and dragged through the streets, made targets of a terrible vendetta by murderous hands; and merely because their crime was to possess a name that was not Chinese?!

Although the revolutionary storm had burst out all over China and future events are still charged with uncertainty and anx-

iety, the Christian benevolence of the Catholic Missions could not remain indifferent to the sufferings of others. So, in a outburst of brotherly love, the mission opened its arms and took the wretched fugitives in, trusting that this act of humanity would be reconciled with a providence which never fails.

Since the Prefecture of Hanchunfu had declared their support for the general revolution, the district Administrator and the Brigadier were compelled to resign, consign their seals of office and abandon the guards to the violence of their new masters; a proceeding that guaranteed their lives, for the time being.

Everyone can imagine not only the humiliation of the disgrace but, even more so, the anxious trepidation in which these ex-authorities were pitched, as they fled without a second thought to the Residence of the Catholic Church, seeking and hoping for a reprieve from further consequences.

But very soon news of alarming events came through to chill hopes of safety. Some troops consisting of a thousand self-styled soldiers from Szechwan, armed to the teeth, were marching on Hanchunfu, and nobody could guess their intentions. To cause even greater alarm, especially to the authorities of the town who had been spared, was the astounding news that an entire army had arrived to occupy the whole department, and so the troops and the new City Council went out, humble and disarmed, to receive… a regiment of rebel partisans! In no time these took possession of the town, demanded money and that the seals of office should be handed over, so that they could legally hold the reins of command.

Now disastrous problems came to light. First came the scarcity of available money because there was barely enough to pay the local allied troops; and second, the use of the seals of office required official confirmation. Naturally, in this case, matters swept to a crisis. It was essential to hold an assembly to discuss the questions which had arisen, with the participation of all parties (including the disarmed local forces).

Among the more important orders of the day was the insidious decision that the ex-authorities, now guests of the Church, should return to the Town for further negotiations. This was clearly a pretext for stripping them of all they possessed and slaughtering them.

Obviously, with this in mind, representatives began to arrive at the Church to demand that our guests be handed over. The latter of course knew full well that once they were outside they would fall

into the hands of executioners, and naturally they energetically refused to obey such an absurd order…

In the thorny controversy that ensued in several days of excited discussion, the Church held firm to its rights, and especially to its duty of charitable love. Finally they succeeded in refusing to comply with the lawless intentions of these arrogant intruders and kept their guests in safety. The townsfolk who were witnesses of these negotiations loudly applauded this shining act of charity.

But the Church's triumphant success had barely become known when the Town was horrified by the killing of the Colonel and the local troops by these self-styled leaders who, expert in extorting money from the prominent citizens of the Town, were now able to get their hands on the arms, ammunition and horses belonging to the local army corps.

However by no means satisfied by so much luck, the partisan regiment now headed off to the Kansu province where, in the first town across the border, they were challenged to a fight with the Muslim citizens who unfortunately were defeated leaving the partisan soldiers free to reap a fat booty in money, horses, etc., and even to round up the children (to sell them to anyone

who wished to adopt them). After this barbaric conquest they returned to Hanchung just at the time when the troops from Sianfu had reached the town. These had been expressly dispatched by the General-in-Chief of the Province to restore order under the new Republican regime.

The moment they heard the news the partisan regiment lost no time in beating a retreat along the road to Szechwan. The ex-authorities of Hanchunfu at the Catholic Mission received the news with a burst of confidence for their safety and at once prepared to return to their distant families. But first they expressed their fervent gratitude to the Italian Catholic Mission, and with infinite prostrations they thanked the Celestial Father for delivering them from such a cruel fate.

The smart and vigorous Brigadier managed to survive a good deal of danger along the way. When he finally reached Peking he hoped to visit the President, Yuen sche Kië, a close friend of his for many years. Tao-tao, who was made of more timid and gentle stuff and already suffering from low morale, was obliged to pass through quite a number of adventures and misfortunes that drove him to the edge of madness. He was completely stripped of all his possessions by highway robbers; even the distinguished decorations he had received in Italy when he was resident there as Chinese Minister were taken from him, although he made every effort to fight back, invoking in his grief the names of Giolitti and Fittoni to come to his aid for such profanation…

Liou…/ Hanchunfu, undated (sheet 1137)

The Revolution in the Southern Shen-Si

A general revolution had first broken out near the province of Szechwan, which had already been undergoing continual tensions owing to the despotism of the local authorities. The first symptoms carried their repercussions almost immediately to our Hanchunfu from October which stirred up panic among the population and serious alarm about what dire events would inevitably follow.

So amid this extreme state of alarm in Hanchunfu, the trends and causes which incited the rebels to revolt and join forces with others who were eager to exterminate the Manchu race, only seemed to be confirmed by the news that came in day by day, and the situation deteriorated hour by hour. Accordingly the major trading posts and small shopkeepers shut down almost at once; the postal service was interrupted and there was no way of knowing anything about events in other parts of the country.

Another element in this first stage of bewildering impressions, was the horror that overcame the population when they heard that young imperial recruits and hordes of partisans had made common cause with the rebels known as Kumintan: masses armed with European rifles who were rushing in to take control of the towns. People who refused to surrender to their programme were hounded into confusion, rounded up and every Manchu amongst them slaughtered with unheard of brutality. Anyone in authority who was Manchu by race or name, or even Chinese loyal to the dynasty, became a marked victim of their anarchic-revolutionary fury, in this holocaust of the Chinese uprising which had already blazed a trail of blood and unreasoning hatred…

Almost unexpectedly Sianfu, capital of the Shen-si, fell victim to one of these towering calamities in the Civil War. For months on end the City became a theatre of blood and horror. The slaughter of 2000 Manchus alone is a macabre page in their history that the revolution's insatiable thirst sealed with its indelible seal of blood and armed plunder…

At chilling news of the kind, one can only imagine the infinite terror that consumed the citizens of Hanchunfu, leaving the local authorities in the utmost anxiety

about what might be in store for them. All the more so because they were afraid of compromising themselves by surrendering to the demands of the revolutionaries: after all Peking could very well repulse the rebels, and the provincial troops of Kan-su might come down and form a resistance. For these reasons they deemed it wiser to focus their efforts on attempting to calm the panic-stricken population.

Amid these turbulent events the Chief Administrator of our Department (Tao-tai) spent wretched days of depression and mortal fear because he is a Manchu by adoption.

The Church remained confident of its immunity, but of course there were no guarantees that it would not have to suffer sudden attacks from the partisans, as well as from the rogues and thieves now turning up in many of the neighbouring districts. In this case the best precaution was to prepare some sort of defence in advance; or at least the appearance of a defence that had a truly providential and magical effect. Some zinc pipes could easily be taken for canons, with tins of Dutch cheese serving as shells. These were placed in the windows of the Residence (in the Town) while Monsignor's crosier, broken in two, was stationed at the front door pointing out at the street to give the impression of two lethal mouths of firearms… In addition to this, I had them carry to the Town gates and wheel through the streets up to the Residence, an acetylene gasometer which fortunately gave the illusion of some fearsome weapon of war which only we Europeans knew how to operate…

It was while these dangers and anxieties possessed the poor Chinese that even worse news was about to break. The Town found it imperative to ensure that it was surrounded with a strong defence to counteract an attack from the bands of partisans, criminals and vandals who had already made havoc of a nearby district, and were said to be on the march towards Hanchunfu.

Primary attention was given to repairing the Town walls which lay in ruins at a number of places. Like almost all Chinese towns the walls ran right around the centre in the form of a quadrilateral. On the outside they were flanked by the remains of a moat which now needed to be re-dug and filled with water.

As the work on the walls was proceeding with alacrity, the iron cannon were dragged out of the town arsenal. For over half a century they had been buried in there rusting with disuse. Mortar shaped, some of them had a calibre of more than

200 mm with a breach about 10 cm thick. These were placed on the so-called cannon terraces which jutted out from the walls on a level with the battlements.

On the four main gates of the Town where the garrison was quartered, some small cannon and iron mortars were mounted while a platoon of armed soldiers kept vigilant watch. Their orders were that anyone entering the Town was to hand them a rock or some stones which they then heaped on the walls for defence.

For many days and nights the blacksmiths had also been sweating over their furnaces, beating out lances, scimitars and long razor sharp knives to supply the Mandarinate, the territorial guards and private citizens. But the supply of iron seemed insufficient for the public needs.

Ever since the first days of conflict and panic, and because of the ever likely invasion of terrorists and robbers, a large section of the population fled to seek refuge in the mountains. I cannot enter into details about this pitiful exodus which would wring the heart of anyone kindly disposed and ready to shed a tear with these suffering people.

On the crests of the nearby mountains and in the hollows of some inaccessible cavern, they built tents out of straw until it resembled a real encampment. There they brought their grain and cereals while they anxiously awaited events, trying to fortify themselves as best as they could. More than half a century before their ancestors had done the same, in the epoch of the invasion of the so-called 'chan-maoz'.

Though picturesque and characteristic, these little national fortresses surrounded by wretched encampments, housed a lowering fear and anguish, to judge by the bewailing and the cursing that echoed from the mountains.

While the Town walls were being fortified, within them there occurred another uprising of the 'new recruits' now stationed there for some months. They went rampaging around the streets, threatening to rebel and to massacre the Mandarin and rob the banks and pawn-shops. It looked as though they were about to join up with the local partisans and perhaps make an attack on the Church. Luckily the situation was fraught with only a few alarms, because the authorities made every effort to suppress and control any attempt at revolt; they tried to maintain public order by the beheading of criminals and stopping further exoduses…

Very soon serious news began to spread through the province: barbaric bands of partisans and criminals, who had done most of the looting and plundering in the skirmishes that ended in the taking of

Sianfu, now turned in the direction of Hanchunfu with more vandalism in mind and showing no respect for the Church. In fact they had destroyed quite a number of churches on their way, just as they had in Fon-sian-fu (in northern Shen-si) where they massacred many Christians, as well as murdering the Mandarins and roasting them over the stoves, not to mention other cruelties and wholesale looting.

As it turned out this imminent danger, that had kept everyone in the utmost anxiety for some days, was completely deviated. At the first signs of disturbance a part of the 'new recruits' together with the local territorial guard were immediately sent to the turn-offs to the mountain roads. There in a narrow ravine, in the range that separates the plains of Sianfu and Hanchunfu, they encountered the bands of rebels. The latter were taken by surprise and were almost entirely slaughtered and beheaded. Their leaders had their hearts and livers cut out to be superstitiously eaten by the conquerors. The heads of the leaders (one was the self-styled King of Hanchunfu) were carried to the authorities in cages as trophies, and exhibited to the public. Naturally, following this timely 'clearance' hopes began to dawn and an air of calm descended, although much remained to be done in the area of security in case of further changes in the situation.

Meanwhile small clandestine republican newspapers began to circulate in the Town. These pompously exalted the glory and conquests of the subversive anti-dynastics, who were gaining new ground day by day. They added new provinces to the Flag, promising, as one might reasonably expect, order and a new regime in favour of the people; at the same time making it clear that they would protect the Church and all Europeans. All this might very well be true, but almost behind them the imperialist troops of Kan-su were being organised to avenge the fate of Sianfu. They were preparing to march there as soon as possible to besiege and reconquer the town by force. Then they intended to come down and protect and defend the Town, which now found itself caught between two fires.

The Church however considered it wiser to remain neutral, always ready to defend itself from any attempt of insurrection on the part of armed robbers and the local partisans as current rumours were suggesting.

In this situation the authorities and other men of position handed over to us their objects of value and once more entrusted their families to the comparative safety of the Church.

By now the question of any kind of defence for the Town gave way before the agreement and union of the provincial troops, the 'new recruits' and the territorial guards of the various districts. So to this effect all weapons were called in and deposited on the parade ground, under the pretext of a military review… The vast parade ground was a magnificent sight. An infinity of bright multicoloured standards and banners fluttered above hundreds of platoons in widely varying dress and arms. Some held rifles, some lances, some daggers and flashing scimitars, as one by one they marched past the official grandstand. In the meantime more bad news suddenly arrived, announcing that the Prefecture of Hinganfu (which was under the administration of Hanchunfu) had rebelled, incited by the neo-revolutionaries, and proclaimed themselves supporters of the general revolution. For some days disorder and tumult reigned, resulting in a number of victims, among them the 80-year-old 'Brigadier' of the Town.

Encouraged by the success of their first strike, and having convinced themselves they were serving the high ideal of saving their country, not perhaps without an eye to plunder, some of the leaders enlisted partisans and criminals and, accompanied by the territorial guards of the neighbouring districts, set off to capture Hanchunfu. Within a few days they had reached the gates of the sub-prefecture of Sisiang (two days from Hanchunfu).

There they burst into the streets with blood-chilling cries of 'kill… kill!' and made directly for the Civil Guard to get their hands on the Mandarin who had narrowly made his escape.

The town gates were closed and very soon they proceeded to their… manipulations, drenching the ground beneath the feet of the terrified townsfolk with blood.

The revolution had won… but the Hanchung authorities instantly sent troops with the territorial guards to avenge and redeem the Town under rebel occupation. First of all they besieged the town, then began the screams, the false attacks, the skirmishes that left behind the dead and wounded, until the town gates were forced open. Amidst all this confusion while the rebels were surrendering, fighting broke out among those who had seized the opportunity for looting… and the soldiers brought the ringleaders of the uprising to prisons and then returned to their barracks while the entire population began to recover from this new incubus that had come to oppress them.

In the aftermath of these dramatic events the situation should have quietened down, yet things suddenly looked blacker than

ever. Again it was the 'new recruits' who showed a certain audacity in wanting to answer the call of their brothers in Sianfu. They were well provided with good European rifles and ammunition, and so naturally, as on many other occasions, they fixed the date of the revolt in the Town. Once again they tried to raise the revolutionary white flag on the walls, and to attack and take the Mandarinate, behead targeted victims… loot the banks and pawn-shops for money…

One day the 'new recruits' not only mutinied but made another attempt on the life of their commanding officer, who luckily escaped and had the delinquents shot and beheaded. From that day on this rabble of undisciplined soldiers, corrupted by every vice, became the bullying bugbear of all the citizens.

While disorder and fear were rife in the town, a detachment of some hundreds of revolutionary soldiers descended from the ravines on the border north of Hanchunfu. They were fleeing the harsh discipline of the general in charge of the metropolis, because after the defeat by the imperialists they deserted and engaged in sacking and looting. The news was given for certain; in fact there was an order from their superiors to immediately arrest and punish the deserters, who thereupon hatched the plan to assault and capture Hanchung (which was still refusing to surrender to the real revolutionaries), and then return to the general in triumph.

This danger seemed even more serious than the ones before. So the best possible defences had to be organised. Two of the Town gates were completely walled up, the other two had to be barricaded with stones and sandbags. The houses built into the wall were the guard posts, and every stretch of the battlements was hung with flags of the various districts of the territorial guards who were there in service. Using every precaution they tried out the canons, already stationed on platforms along the wall. One reconnaissance patrol marched against the enemy, who avoided them by using another mountain road which opened out abruptly onto to the plain. The enemy met with practically no serious resistance on their march because they employed a subtle tactic with the population, and so they halted and waited near a large village where the territorial guard was stationed, about two hours from the gates of Hanchunfu.

At such a short distance, battle became inevitable, given the insidious aims of the enemy and the defence of the Town which stood firm in its resolution to fight back with all the forces the authorities could muster, now that they were confident of

success. As soon as the rebels struck camp they were suddenly roused to confront an attack from thousands of men of the territorial guard. After frantic resistance under fire from European rifles, they were forced to beat a retreat because they were betrayed and only equipped with traditional weapons.

In the mean time everything was organised for resistance on the walls of the Town. The bastions swarmed with men with whatever arms they could lay hands on, watching through the crenels of the battlements. It was forbidden to leave or enter the Town and, since the gates were blocked, only couriers or people of trust could be hauled up or let down on ropes. Men suspected of spying or betrayal were instantly beheaded, a without a trial…

Nightfall came slowly and ominously silent on that stormy day. The Brigadier assembled his soldiers, exhorted them and sent them into battle, promising each a reward if they returned victorious. These were joined by the 'new recruits' who were now proclaiming their allegiance. As the soldiers marched out there was almost a sensation of relief, together with the hope that the enemy would be held back, or at least find it impossible to scale the walls. The Town was wrapped in darkness and a hubbub of anxious whispering. On every battlement along the wall paper lanterns and oil lamps were lit. Myriads of little lights flickering in the winter breeze created an air of festivity beneath the soft radiance of the stars.

Everyone stood at his post on the bastions atop the walls. The Brigadier with his rusty battery stood at the forefront above the East Gate. The Chief Administrator of the Department (kao tao) occupied the North gate with his garrison; the Prefect and the Vice Prefect, respectively, at the South and West gates. The watchword passed from one ear to the next. Eyes peered into the darkness and every ear was pricked for the least sound. Everywhere a tranquil silence reigned…

Towards midnight the Town was shaken by a burst of rifle and canon fire. Then a short silence. From the walls and inside the Town came a blast, a torrent of screams and yells at such a pitch that the sensation remained with me for a good ten days. The uproar was created by panic-stricken citizens who thought the rebels had entered the Town. Then half an hour later the pandemonium of yelling and screaming died away. The reason for all this alarm was that a few of the enemy had crept to the wall and asked to be pulled up on the ropes. Obviously the answer was a volley of rifle shot which sent them racing back into the darkness.

Similarly, other noises could be heard near the walls and figures of men made out. There was another burst of rifle fire, immediately followed by a menacing unison of 'kill… kill…' at the pitch of their lungs, that was instantly picked up and imitated by the defenders of the Town. The enemy tried in vain to scale the walls at a number of places, but since they were always driven back, suffering losses, they took to their heels at sunrise, while our soldiers re-entered the Town with booty and prisoners. The latter were decreed expiatory victims for 'human sacrifice'. On the same day an altar was erected in one of the squares, surmounted by a 'commemorative plaque' dedicated to the old Commander of the territorial guard who had been treacherously butchered by the rebels (they ate his heart after gouging out his eyes).

The prisoners were led before the altar, their hands tied behind their backs; then two incense candles were lit, whereupon the prisoners were quartered alive; next they had their hearts cut out and these, still beating and fuming, were delivered up to the Brigadier who offered them with great dignity to the spirit of the great Commander as a cruel token of vendetta…

The disbanded rebels once again reorganised themselves to attempt another massacre. In this perilous situation the provincial troops who had set out on reconnaissance returned just in time. An offensive was now planned, namely to turn on the rebels, decimate them and pursue the others as far as possible. Consequently we endured more days of attacks and guerrilla skirmishes, with more dead and wounded, until finally the rebels were chased back into the mountains bordering on Szechwan. In one of their last retreats a faction of the rebels tried to make for our Residence in Culupa. Their idea was to capture our European canons (which we do not have) and with these return to take possession of our Town… However while we were still seriously alarmed, the territorial guard, organised on a voluntary basis from the nearby pagan villages, were more than a thousand fully armed men. They suddenly rushed to the hill of Culupa to place themselves at our defence and to block the advance of the rebels, who now deemed it more prudent to change plans and make off as fast as possible.

This event is a sure tangible sign of unfailing divine protection towards out Italian Vicariate, since the Culupa Residence, the various buildings of our schools and charitable work, as well as the orphanages of the Canossian nun, had no more than 50 people for defence, 8 European missionaries and the Vicar Apostolic who was taken seriously ill at this time. To defend the Residence in Hanchung, the orphanage and buildings under construction, we were four missionaries, and in case of need we had about forty old but well-armed soldiers, whom the Colonel had placed at our disposal.

The fact is that throughout the various bloody and horrifying phases of the revolution we ourselves suffered no brutal incidents or misfortunes. I should add that we were even surrounded by warm friendship and respect. So we should thank Our Father in Heaven for His presence, His comfort and protection and how He listened to and granted the innocent pleas of the thousands of children in our orphanages.

After such terrible events, which held the population in the grip of fear for months on end, the moment a little peace and calm returned, plots were already being hatched against the authorities themselves while the population was threatened with an internal revolt.

Now the 'new recruits' were no longer alone, and proved and irresistible force. In fact, shortly before the old Chinese year was out, they finally planted the longed for flag of the revolution on the walls and on all the buildings, without a single complaint or serious incident. However the Chief Administrator of the Department and the Brigadier, were not only removed from office and forced to hand over the so-called 'seals' of imperial investiture, but were expelled from their respective seats of power.

The new year (4610 dating from the reign of the first Emperor of China) marked to the world the death throes of the Manchu dynasty and the rise to power of the Chinese people…
Hanchunfu, 1912 (sheet 1134)

The First Anniversary of the Chinese Republic

After a whirlwind of feverish events the Chinese Republic has finally come to the end of its first year of compounding all its heterogeneous elements. In spite of the tumultuous and dire disorder of the revolution whose painful and awesome echoes still reverberate to this day, the bold young republicans have felt the need to give vent to their joy in singing the glories of victory, and enthusiastically hailing the dawn of the first anniversary of the infant Republic.

So nothing could be more fitting than to celebrate the spirit of progress, which has launched the re-flowering and re-emergence of the present fortunes of this vast and stricken country, whose future for-

tunes are safeguarded by courageous and fervent champions with high hopes for their country…

As in all the other provinces, the memorable date of the annexation of their own towns to republican reform, Hanchung has also participated in the patriotic three-day jubilation. All the towns are festively decorated. There is no longer the old 'yellowing dragon' banner, but their own national 'five-colour' flag fluttering for the first time from on high, mingling harmoniously with the myriads of floral lanterns which create such a fantastic and brilliant effect at nightfall. The narrow streets, thronging with deafening swarms of merchants and pedestrians have become long lane-ways decorated with slender arches, pennants and streamers and Chinese lanterns, all in silk and cloth and paper in bright, vividly contrasting colours. At the entrance of the Mandarinates and public buildings stood two national flags with a double row of streamers attached to the edges representing the flags of all the European nationalities.

The official festival was held separately in the Mandarinates, barracks and the meeting room of the committees of the National Assembly. The 'Lieutenant-General', together with all the officers of Military Headquarters, wearing their rows of decorations for grand occasions, reviewed the permanent troops on the parade ground of the capital of the Prefecture. The members of the various town councils or 'Committees of the National Assembly' from all the villages of any importance, were brought together to hold short speeches and addresses, congratulating all concerned on the present state of things, and wishing the new nation every prosperity. Some of them spoke of the decadence caused by opium addiction and stigmatised the unhygienic and useless pigtail; some deplored the custom of binding women's feet, while others urged the necessity for new reforms. In short they spoke of all the matters that would necessarily and automatically facilitate the welfare and standard of living in the country. In all of this there was an obvious imitation of Europe, not to mention a call for caution.

What with conversations of the new kind, the enthusiastic flourish of flags and banners and the fantastic nocturnal illuminations; the banquets which saw a mania for the raising of hats and the shaking of hands, and a proud flaunting of European hats and shoes… it seemed that ancestors were laughed out of court as the festival went its merry way.

But what can we say about the people?! They have always been accustomed to

observe an indifference more ironic than heroic. They are still full of fatalistic presentiments and pessimism which, psychologically speaking, is difficult to diagnose. It is true they are only too glad to run like puppets after any charlatan buffoon, blind to any real sensation and ready to laugh and cry with him… but the laughter rings grotesque and evil.
Hanchungfu, 1912

Customs and Practices

Notes on Marriage
In the year 1903 the parents of Leao-tzun found a likely match for their son in the person of the daughter of a certain Cun, and through the good offices of a marriage broker, the consent of both sets of parents was granted and finalised. They also established the day when, according to custom, the young man was to go and see his future bride; in fact it was the only time the young couple had an opportunity to meet both before and after the ceremony. But he first beheld his future bride the young man immediately noticed the defect of her feet (a part of the body to which the Chinese attach major importance in assessing a woman's beauty). Indeed her feet were extremely large; that is to say, not narrowly bound up from babyhood to form a very small foot, according to the Chinese practice and custom. The young man was highly incensed and immediately turned on his heel and walked straight home heedless of the teeming rain.

His parents however were quite poor, and they urged and insisted that their son should gladly accept the girl. Moreover, they said, since they all lived in the mountains hardly anyone would notice the defect in her feet. And, after all, since it was good match financially they would be able to invite the bride to the house with very little expense. But the son stood firm on his decision never to have that girl for his wife. But in the mean time the parents exchanged gifts on both sides and the marriage was concluded in the sense that the girl could be 'invited' (as a sort of acquisition or its equivalent) with three lengths of cloth.

But then a doubt was raised as to whether the girl had already been promised in another marriage to her father's adopted son, who had since fled the house. As a result when the girl was sent to the orphanage the parish priest looked into the matter. Asking for information from Kan-su, the girl's birthplace, and receiving the news that there was no existing impediment, the reluctant bridegroom was called to Culupa (i.e., to the orphanage) so that the couple could be united in holy

wedlock… And who was there who knew that the 'groom' was so fiercely against the marriage?! However his sisters-in-law at home and his parents continually urged and insisted, so that for better or worse they were sure he would end up by agreeing… In fact, after a call from Culupa (the Bishop's Residence) the young man duly presented himself with his elder brother. He was taken to the nuns' chapel (a normal procedure) and there the sacred rite was performed. It is true he happened to pronounce the tremendous 'I do'. Besides, finding himself before a parish priest, he was powerless to do what his heart and his urge for freedom told him. He was afraid he would threatened, punished and beaten if he hesitated a single moment. So he let others do what they liked in their own house, while in his own house he put his freedom first. The moment he arrived home again the bride with the long feet was 'invited'. Banquets were prepared and friends and members of the family were asked for the celebration. Everything that Chinese etiquette demanded on these occasions was carried out to the last detail. But all the while the groom did not utter a word, or spare a glance towards the girl he had refused from the bottom of his heart the very first time he set eyes on her,. He had decided she would never be his and never share his bed, and from the day of the nuptials they separated like strangers. As long as I live, he said, even if I remain a bachelor, she will not be mine; I do not want her; take her to Culupa (the orphanage) to live as a virgin because I shall never touch her at any price.

And so matters remained for nearly five years, while they both lived in the father's house, but forever separated. His parents and sisters-in-law now began to grumble much more when they saw that the unfortunate bride did absolutely nothing at all, and was totally incapable of coping with the simplest household tasks. She was a sort of doll without any thought (for herself or others'?). One day, or rather late at night while the rain was pouring down outside, the bride dressed herself in her new clothes and disappeared from the house. Discovering her absence the next morning, the family sent out people to look for her, but found no trace. Later on, an express arrived from the nearby mission (20 kilometres) and the parish priest called the young man to come and see him immediately. The boy went. At his first contact with the priest he felt as if he were tightly bridled like a horse, and that his legs were too swollen to walk. In short he could hardly move for the swelling and the pain, and the fact that he still had no idea of what it was all about. But then he heard that it concerned his runaway wife who had turned up at a Residence with her clothes torn and then been taken to Culupa. So now he was obliged to go with the parish priest and was sure to be given the punishment he deserved. The caravan departed and our young man was accompanied by two police officers. On the way he made the excuse he wanted to stop for a 'call of nature' and, permission granted, he took to his heels as fast as he could. Three or four days later he reached his home to tell them of his sad adventure. But one of the men acting as policeman, a Christian as it turned out, sent public officers to the boy's house to bring him back. However, it was said, that since they were Christians the boy's father decided to go himself to the parish priest. The next day other police officers arrived and put the poor boy in chains. The villagers, who were both Christian (3 or 4 families) and pagan […] knew very well how matters stood: they were outraged by this procedure, and in fact wanted to fight the clear injustice; they would have sent the public officers to another world had the boy's father not intervened to vouch for them. The officers claimed that the parish priest wanted the fugitive brought before him. Well, said the father, I shall go to the parish priest myself. The poor old man spent quite a few sapeks to get to the priest's house, only to find that he had been spending the last few days in Culupa. The father immediately saw that the summons was an invention to squeeze more money from him, and made the long trip back swallowing his anger. From that day on, three whole years, the bride with the big feet remained at the orphanage, while her young husband stayed in his father's house tilling the soil. The property and the family house was divided up and Leao-tzun's share was more than 40 tiao (about 120 lire), with 20 tiao in ready money to keep the girl at the orphanage until he was forced into taking her away. In that case, he said, he had good strong legs to run away from the girl with the long feet…

This whole story sounds like a novel, but it is pure fact: a historical novel with characters sill living. For years they have been hoping for grace and aid to keep them from ruin. Punishments and unconfessed secrets, things suggesting perversion and abandonment, ending with the renunciation of sacred vows.

Undated (sheet 1125)

From China: a bell that… flies!

No need to turn up your noses, you aviation fans!… the bell I want you to meet no longer flies. But once it did fly. At least that is what the Chinese of our Hanchungfu, who live in a world of fantasy and dream, will tell you. And tell you they will, a thousand times; and so seriously in fact that one can only seriously lament their so deeply superstitious sentimentality.

They are more than convinced that on one still and serene night the bell of Hanchungfu went for its clandestine flight with a 'male' bell. Their silent journey was lit only by twinkling starlight. The pure and limpid air proudly carried this mysterious couple on its gleaming wings of iridescent dew. Lightly they furrowed the ethereal pathways with an imposing majesty that instilled reverence and awe in the wandering spirits when it reached the North gate of the town of Hanchung-fu. Here she paused awhile before lowering herself down on ropes of pearls and diamonds by the door of a pagoda. In fact she descended a little too far, just 3 inches too low, burying her rim in the earth. At the time when 'long-haired barbarians' were about to burst into the town, the 'male' bell made off, leaving his lady in despair. The 'barbarians' saw her as prize booty and dug around her, but… the more they dug the more the bell sank even deeper into the earth, bringing their wicked designs to naught…

This is why the townsfolk of Hanchung, who wanted the bell themselves, recount the origins of their town. They admire their bell and continually tell the story. They are immensely proud of this beautiful bell made entirely of bronze, flecked here and there with streaks of silver and decorated with splendid raised reliefs and with a superb, finely wrought group of intertwined dragons on the upper part. In fact the decoration looks as though it was chiselled by the hand of a fairy.

In the course of time, for what reason no one can tell but probably the result of the lamentations of the bell itself, a crack opened on one side. Thereupon the most devout, in their religious hearts, believed that they should come to her aid by burning leaves in supplication and light little candles to placate some tremendous vendetta…

The crack naturally widened until it assumed the shape of a stove door, and evil hands even tried to reach in and prise off the streaks of silver.

As it turned out the bell had no further reason to complain after so much magical consolation, and down to this day she has remained there, frozen in her widowed corner, in a silence broken only by visits from iher dear friends…

She does not lament her fate, nor does she dream of making a second flight, because she knows full well that her wings are… clipped!

Hanchungfu, September 1911 (sheet 1039)

Lioyang and the Chandelier of Freedom

The enchanting town of Lioyang on the border of the extreme west of Hanchung-fu, enjoys such a picturesque position that it is impossible not to be fascinated by the magnificent view. Gently poised on the slope of a hill that extends out of sight among an interminable chain of mountains, like a celestial peninsular it is lapped all around by the crystal waters of two mountain streams and the turgid yellow waters of a navigable river.

Unfortunately the walls, though once unassailable, are now largely destroyed and are continually menaced by the churning and roaring of flood waters. This is a constant source of anxiety to the citizens who are compelled to seek refuge in the nearby mountains.

From the very first the precarious condition of the town's water situation was a matter of keen concern for the ancestors who met to discuss it and eventually devised the project to erect a prayer tower, which exists to this day on the mountain facing the town. The tower was dedicated to the goddess Coan-în, so that she would protect the townsfolk from the fury of the floods.

Last year however the Lightning God blasted the top of the tower and deeply injured the plump shoulders of the goddess herself. Later, with funds from the imperial treasury, a new supplementary town was built but it remains uninhabited and precarious for lack of maintenance. What meets the eye inside the town is the agglomerate of a confused and fantastic multicoloured mosaic of houses, Mandarinates and pagodas, some them authentic monuments of the ancient classical Chinese style.

The excessive abuse of opium and the enormous increase in tolls are causing the collapse of customs and beggaring trade and local industry once of distinguished repute.

Another marvel for the traveller and a prodigious talisman for the citizens of Lioyang is the heavy wrought iron chandelier in the form of a globe and pendent, also spherical, an exquisite interweaving of flowers and leaves that hangs in the temple of the guardian spirit.

This elegant chandelier is an authentic and unequalled masterpiece for the Chinese, and never to be separated from the moving story of the genius who created it. He was a blacksmith who was arrested and imprisoned for some serious offence. The court and the supreme inquisition, who made their annual adamant decisions, sentenced him to capital punishment which struck the poor blacksmith in the heart like an arrow of fire.

After his panic had quietened the blacksmith decided to ask for a few days grace, telling them he wanted to consecrate a work worthy of his genius, and so magnificent that it would not only immortalise his name but gain him an imperial pardon and liberation.

He began at once with a glowing ardour to forge two identical chandeliers, one of them to be sent to the supreme court as pledge of his word. The chandelier aroused a widespread wonder and admiration and everyone declared it a matchless work that only one genius could create. The blacksmith's hopes were fulfilled and he won his freedom.

It sounds much like a legend and yet it is partly confirmed by another similar case that occurred recently. A man of letters, doomed to the fatal scimitar the following morning, spent his last night making a desperate mental effort to dictate a volume in which all the Chinese characters are grouped, and whose classical elegance and mastery earned him the boon of freedom.

Hanchungfu, September 1911 (sheet 1048)

The 'Postal Chimneys' in China, 1914

Anyone who has had the good fortune to travel through the interior of China, so attractive with its original features that can only be found in the Far East, will certainly have noticed that all the houses of all the populations have no chimneys, and for this reason China has been called the land without chimneys.

However if we trace back to some centuries ago, history assures us that under the stormy rule of a perverse dynasty, the serious and precarious conditions of those times challenged the wits of the ancestors of the day and they came up with the idea of building some 'smoking aerials' (yen-huo-töèn); that is, special chimneys which would serve only for transmitting imperial dispatches over long distances, or else orders of the utmost urgency in the threat of public calamity. These 'postal chimneys', which were taller than any of the tall houses, were simply built of mud, shaped either as a pyramid or cone, whitewashed on the outside, and with small furnace at the foot. These 'chimney stacks' spread throughout the principal points of every province and district, ramifying from one to the next at intervals of 5 ly. They resembled a battle line of white pinnacles trailing through China until they reached the imperial capital in Peking.

Every 'postal chimney' was annexed with a house for the 'postal guards', whose express duty it was to keep at readiness for every occasion, a certain amount of fuel for the 'chimney' which had to be burnt the moment the signal was seen. The fuel consisted of wolves' excrement, which, according to the Chinese, is the only kind that will give off a thick column of smoke, and keeps straight and compact as it rises to a very great height.

This invention was intended to represent a great service to the Empire but it worked out rather badly for the emperor who was the first to use it to warn the people of the Tibetan and Mongol invasions. Although delighted when the 'postal chimneys' were completed, the emperor then turned much more of his attention, and his heart, to the multitude of women who commanded the court, but not to his people.

The Chinese relate that after many centuries the Emperor Thu-yu-wan was one day standing on the turret of his roof, which appeared to be carpeted with shining green and gold enamel tiles looking like fleets of small gondolas. Before him, on a lacquered tray, the scented steam of a teapot wove a flickering halo around the young and exceptionally beautiful face of the empress. 'Well, my Paô-së, when will you allow my eyes to see your vermilion lips parted in a smile?!' Now although Paô-së was surrounded by everything that could possibly give her delight she had never once smiled upon her lord. However at that moment she was struck by an extravagant idea; she stopped to gaze at the files of white 'postal chimneys' which spread away across the land and beyond the horizon. Then she pointed to them and asked what they were for. The emperor was quick to tell her what she wished. 'Give orders that all the fires in the 'smoking antennas' be lighted and you shall have what you wish from me', replied Paô-së, almost in a tone of prayer. The emperor immediately gave the order and the 'postal chimneys' promptly transmitted their signal. Behind each one there was a desperate flurry and scattering of military Mandarins at he head of their soldiers in full battle dress, all convinced that the capital was in the grip of danger. And it was then, when she saw this vast multitude running up from all over the empire, that Paô-së laughed heartily, filling the heart of the emperor with joy and he could not help telling his expectant armies all about it. The joke did not go down so well with the soldiers who

exchanged dark glances at having been made fools of for the sake of a smile, and went their ways home cursing Paô-së.

It was a very different story however when the rebels marched in the take the capital, while the panic-stricken emperor called for help by lighting the 'postal chimneys'. Everyone heard about the signal but no one moved a step, fearing it yet another of the emperor's jokes, and both the capital and the emperor fell into the hands of the rebels.

Alas, these days when we look across the centuries down to the last unhappy dynasty, we find other Paô-sës who have dragged the 'Celestial Empire' into a fearsome cycle of convulsions and disorder, both civil and moral. The 'postal chimneys' we still see here and there, mute and abandoned, stand like memorials of an ironic silence, scarcely daring to speak of the wickedness of times gone by.
Hanchungfu, 1914 (sheet 1099)

Crafts and Trades

Bamboo Paper and its Preparation

Virgin forests abound in wild bamboo, which normally never reaches the height and thickness of cultivated bamboo. In spring, before the leaves have unfurled from their delicate sheaf, all the new and still tender plants are collected.

To do this, groups of men women and children are to be found scattered through the gorges and on mountain tops cutting the green bamboo which they tie into bundles and carry back to the paper mill. At this time of the year the mountains ring with shouting, monotonous chanting, etc. etc.

At the paper mill the bundles of bamboo are left to macerate in a basin of still water which gradually evaporates in the sun leaving the canes putrefied but still firm and fibrous.

As soon as the paper mill has acquired enough bamboo to last for a year of processing, they proceed to crush the previously softened bamboo; this is a job for the old men and children who beat the canes with wooden hammers, reducing the tougher fibre. Then the stems are graded and the longest are folded into smaller but very light bundles, while the short ones and the fragments are also bundled and tied in the form of a X, then carried to a sort of basin near the paper mill.

In another outside place nearby, the bamboo bundles are neatly piled, then sprayed with slaked lime. For this job special workers are taken on because the good quality of the paper depends on knowing how much slaked lime to use, otherwise an excessive amount would burn the

material and make it unusable; just as an insufficient amount would be useless and waste time spent on further processing. So many in the trade have been ruined by some worker who miscalculates the right amount of lime, either through inexperience or because the overseers have been stingy with his wages!

When the bundles of bamboo have absorbed enough slaked lime and lost much of their fibrous content, which happens over a period varying up to one month, they are packed neatly but not too tightly in a large wooden tub bound with hoops of bamboo, about 4 metres in diameter and 10 metres deep. This placed over a large iron boiler filled with water, about 3 metres in diameter, and set into a specially dug ditch. When the vat is full ,or rather overfilled, because the pile of bamboo rises about 4 metres above the level of the rim of the vat a fire is lit in the furnace below the boiler, and great care taken to see that the bundles of bamboo above it are enveloped only by the steam. This operation could very well be called a steam bath. A blazing fire is kept alight by the addition of more wood and the evaporated water is replaced.

As is fairly obvious, the action of the steam on the lime-soaked fibre of the bamboo softens and detaches all the fibrous cells; so that the huge pile of bundles sinks lower and lower until it forms a homogeneous mass. At this point a hollow is made in the mass using a cane with iron hooks; with this the bundles at the bottom of the vat can be scooped up to the top, allowing the mass to be uniformly exposed to the steam bath. All this takes about a fortnight, after which the mass of bamboo (now called canapa) is removed from the vat and taken to a large but shallow bath nearby that is continually supplied from the torrents in the adjacent gorges. Here a thorough washing of the whole mass is carried out with pitchforks for 7 days, until all the slaked lime is removed.

The fibrous mass is placed in another cistern, buried 4 metres deep and 3 metres wide in the ground nearby, and with a solid boiler open to the sky, above which some small beams are arranged and a row of strong canes to form a grating, i.e. a diaphragm of bamboo canes. Next a soda lye obtained from an extract of the buckwheat plant is poured in. The fire beneath the boiler is kept burning day and night, but the water should not be allowed to reach boiling point. From time to time the mass is stirred, adding more water as it evaporates during the boiling. After a number of days (7), enough to for the bamboo fibre to separate out, the whole

mass is taken out and once again placed in the big vat, though without washing it, and given another steam bath. After another seven days it is washed again for a few days, then once again arranged in the cistern, only this time in strata, i.e. one stratum of bamboo fibre onto which is poured a fermented liquid of rice and one of pulses, then another stratum of fibre and another of liquid, and so on for many strata until the cistern is completely filled. Below it a slow fire is made and kept burning for about ten days. At this point the fibre is reduced to the state of a threadbare rag, a rather sticky one. Now the bamboo paste is ready to be transformed into pages and placed in a store house.

In another part of the mill covered with straw, windowless and therefore in semidarkness with no signs of cleaning or tidiness, we find the workers ready to perform the final operation in the process. The paste, so treated, is brought to this room and placed into a sort of wooden triangle, where the bottom and the walls are covered with a thick network of bamboo, and where two or more people are pressing and squeezing the paste. It is then poured into a wooden tub with a double bottom, i.e. with a diaphragm of bamboo, and filled with water underneath. The paste is continually pounded and minced and worked from one side to the other. Finally the water is removed from the vat below so that only the paste remains. This is then transferred to other more commodious basins, one for each worker. Into these wooden basins just over half the water is poured, plus two or even three buckets of paste, according to the quantity needed, and finally a bucket of gummy water obtained from the macerated roots of a wild plant, 'iow Agër'.

Now both skilled and unskilled workers stir the watery mass with a stiff brush. Next they take a wooden framework equipped with two handles, upon which is placed a very fine bamboo grating, the size of the page of paper required. It looks a little like a piece of matting and must be very carefully varnished to prevent the paste from sticking. They then pass this once or twice into the mixture; on opening the handles they remove the 'matting' onto which a very thin gauzy stratum is deposited, which soon settles on a wooden panel of the same size.

This operation needs to be carried out with the greatest possible care because it is on this that the thickness and uniformity of the paper depends; so it must be performed with the utmost skill and efficiency by experienced workers. The pages of paper, still wet, are laid out very precisely one on top of the other; there is no danger they will stick. When the pile of pages reaches an approximate number, calculated by the height of the pile, they are brought to the press in the same workroom, and pressed until all the water has been expelled and the pages are almost dry. The packs of pages are then taken to another part of the mill, built in long cells intersected by a long oven with thin triangular walls. Wood is continually kept burning in the oven, so that the outside walls are heated to a constant even temperature, around 42 degrees; here, on these heated walls, the pages are placed to dry in a very short time.

Finally packs of paper are made up of six reams, 10 pages to a ream, and taken to the store room where other workers submit the packs to the press, smooth out the wrinkled edges with a maize stalk, and bind them with strips of bamboo. The name and stamp of the firm is affixed and day porters carry the packs to the shop in the nearby town for sale to merchants at the weekday fair, etc.

From China, 1911 (sheet 1063)

Cormorant Fishing
on the Han River in China

There can be no doubt about fishing. It is an amusing past-time and has always had its attractions, especially because it has always retained a certain simplicity by way of gear.

Things are much the same in China where, in the interior alone, there are quite a number of rivers, large and small, lakes, and rice paddies, all enlivened with people fishing; an everyday event because there is an abundance of fish of every species.

However to get a good marketable supply the shrewd and industrious Chinese fisherman does not stop at using a line, hook and nets. He had many other methods at his command, sometimes as curious as they are simple.

One of these is fishing with cormorants, or 'sea crows' which the Chinese also call 'siù-lâo-uá', or 'water crows'.

Fishermen on the shores of northern Europe dread this sea bird because of the great inroads it makes on their fishing capacities; but if Chinese fishermen go out for an abundant catch they cannot do without cormorants, which they raise and domesticate with a loving care; I would go so far to say, almost religiously. In fact a good cormorant can be worth 20 ounces of silver (50 francs) with a performance expectation of decades.

Normally every fisherman plies his trade quite freely and for his own benefit, and in any time of the year without licence or taxation from the authorities, who however enjoy the right of paying half price on any kind of catch.

Once or twice a year, according to local practice, more and more fishermen gather together and settle on a certain stretch of the river where they are going to make their big haul. This can last for more than three months, particularly if the they agree on the last three months of autumn, i.e. shortly after the rainy season when the rivers are still in flood.

The fishing boats are rather small (especially as they have to serve as lodgings and kitchen for three or four people). Each is equipped with nets, harpoons, iron hooks and pikes, etc., as well as some light, narrow, spear-shaped canoes with dimensions of 3 metres long, 50 cm wide and 40 cm deep; these dimensions vary with the number of cormorants available.

Four cormorants for every canoe manned by one person; a long bamboo cane that does the job of a paddle, two bamboo baskets and a pike with a long handle: this is all the equipment they need.

Let us leave behind the curious crowd of lookers-on lining the river banks and follow our fishermen (after they ritually light a candle to their protecting idol and sacrifice a cock, smearing the boats with its blood in high hopes). Some of the fishermen are repairing nets, some tying strings to the necks of the cormorants which already bear identification marks on their wings or tail.

Anyone witnessing these preparations and the whole course of events of an expedition like this, would enjoy the sight of a tiny flotilla, sailing gaily off to encounter... the harmless fish!

A shout is raised at the departure and the slender canoes slide into the centre of the river, twisting and turning among the confusion of the canoes of other fishermen who incite their starving and croaking cormorants to plunge into the waves...

The hungry green-eyed cormorant has spotted his prey and in a flash scoops it up in its infallible and terrible beak, bringing it to the surface of the water, while the vigilant fisherman is waiting with his hook to draw in both fish and cormorant; after this the bird makes another dive...

Sometimes grim struggles occur beneath the water when the prey is a 20 pounder or more, or else one of the big river tortoises. When this happens the cormorants help one another to prevent the prey from escaping. But if the fisherman does not come to the rescue in time the cormorant may tire and abandon its prey.

It could also happen, though rarely, that when the string has been removed from the cormorant's neck it may overeat on small fishes, and not only forget its duty but, unless its wings are clipped, it might suddenly decide to fly off on its own and abandon the river.

The most sought-after places for fishing are the shoals, where the canoes turn around and around while nets are cast from fishing boats in the targeted area. Fishing by this method never lasts longer than a few hours a day but, on the other hand, with a collection of some fifty cormorants, a big or small catch can vary up to two thousand pounds in weight.

So the cormorants must not only be well nourished, on a daily ration of about 3 pounds of fish and a sort of 'loaf' called tô-fu,[2] but (and this may seem strange) when its beak is opened it must be given a drink since it cannot drink in the river when its neck is tied.

So here, gentle reader, the cormorants live a dependent life to the advantage of the Chinese fishermen. Ocean going fishermen may find some consolation in the thought that by transforming these dangerous sea birds into winged assistants they will certainly reap a greater catch and no doubt have fun doing it.

9 May 1909 (sheet 1145)

[2] The Chinese use tô-fu as an everyday inexpensive dish. It is a sort of soft white 'loaf' of a thick consistency, obtained from a heated coagulation of vegetable casein and starch converted into dextrin and glucose, previously separated through the maceration and mincing of pulse seeds (e.g. soya).

Mission

An Italian Representative
in Southern Shen-Si

Last summer the Italian Apostolic Viacariate of southern Shen-Si (annexed two years ago to the Italian protectorate) was honoured by a representative of the Royal Italian Legation in Peking, in the person of the Illustrious Cavalier M. Bensa.

At a place situated in the heart of the Chinese Empire and still closed to relations with Europe, such an event is not only rare but even unique.

Without wishing to detail the precise reasons for the visit, diplomatic or no, let me say that Italy can be proud to embark on such a relation, however delicate it may be given all the possible susceptibilities in regard to persons and things. However we strongly believe that as far as Italo-Chinese relations are concerned Italian prestige will not only emerge more substantial in political forms, but will obtain a still more concrete benefit, particularly in the protection of Italian nationals and missionaries resident in China, and also in the development of trade.

The festive and expansive welcomes, for the illustrious representative was received with all honours, resounded with a courtesy and cordiality that is quite Italian. In fact the Vicar Apostolic, Monsignor Pio G. Passerini and all the missionaries resident here were unanimous in bestowing this deservedly appreciated tribute.

The local authorities, both civil and military, gave expression to all the ancient and sumptuous etiquette, both by their presence and in their receptions, as well as the reciprocal visits and customary formal banquets. So that the illustrious guest, our Italian Legate, was surrounded with all due honour.

By far the most enjoyable and intimate occasion was held in the Orphanage attached to the principal Residence of Culupa, and run by the meritorious Canossian nuns who for many years have offered a helping hand and sacrificed the flower of their lives for the moral and material good of hundreds of poor innocent girls, whose increasing numbers reflect their increasing rejection by inhuman pagan parents. As a prelude to the improvised feast, some little girls dressed in white, red and green, recited a poetic address, in Italian, in the presence of the representative.

This was followed by gymnastic displays accompanied by the singing of Italian songs, performed separately by children of all ages, from the eldest down to the very small. This tiny female army gave happy proof of their success and drew a resounding and sincere applause together with heartfelt admiration for the Casnossian nuns who had organised such an enjoyable occasion and with admirable care and patience.

The Vicariate of southern Shen-Si was built twenty-five years ago after the foundation in Rome of the Pontifical Seminary for Foreign Missions which received the name of the munificent founder, Pius IX of sacred memory.

Almost every year young priests emerge from the Seminary and bid farewell to their families and their Italian homeland. They go to join their brother missionaries, willing to accept every hardship and sacrifice in spreading Religion, thereby bringing men nearer to God and giving that first impulse to an authentic civilization. In the brief course of this last period they have been working tirelessly to build new secondary Residences in order to expand in new directions and gain a wider field for conversion to Christianity.

Now it is to be hoped that they can proceed to other projects already prepared, but still awaiting the necessary participation and help from […].

Geographically, the little known region of southern Shen-Si can be found at 104-116 degrees longitude and between 31 and 34 degrees latitude. It is surrounded in the north by the Tesin mountains (?) which mark the border of northern Shen-Si, east of the Hupe province, south of Setzuan and west of Banzu. As for climate, it is fairly wet for most of the year, with vast plains under rice cultivation, and also because of the periodic annual rainfall.

The richness of the country is mainly due to the number of rivers whose waters are a prime necessity for the maintenance of the rice paddies. The river Hou alone, that originates in this area, is not only a boundless source of fish, but creates and assures mercantile trade as far as Hankoro.

The population not only work at the cultivation of rice, which is daily bread for the Chinese, but intensifies its industry in small-scale trading; and producing a variety of their own local products, that are also exported outside the province.

This, in brief, is the province of Shen-Si where Italy wished to send its illustrious representative like a second Marco Polo. These brief notes will serve to inform the benevolent reader, that beyond the seas and in the midst of the huge Chinese Empire, a small group of Italians live and sacrifice themselves for the cause of Christian redemption, to the glory of the Church and our beloved Homeland.

Undated (sheet 1143)

Tao-Tâi among the Italian Missionaries in Culupa

Recently the new local Prefect Hoan Kâo was an unexpected and very welcome guest at the Residence of the Vicar Apostolic, which lies in an intriguingly undulating landscape of green hills, 70 ly from the Prefecture town of Hanchungfu. The new Prefect arrived in a litter accompanied by a formal train of followers and the civil Mandarin of the territory.

After the usual reception, following established etiquette, he visited the interior of the Residence, the Cathedral, the female orphanage where the children offered him a collective recitation, and all the other buildings dedicated to various charitable activities in which the missionaries are presently engaged. The Prefect had little expected works on this scale and was most enthusiastic, unable to refrain from praise and appreciation of the buildings and the humanitarian activities they housed, entirely for the benefit of his abandoned people.

As the new Tao-Tâi had been living for some time in Rome as Chinese Minister to the Italian Government, he naturally wished to tell us about how he received the cross of Cavaliere which he was wearing. He also gave us his impressions and memories of people he met in Italy and the wonderful things he saw there. Probably his stay in Italy had considerably refined him and taught him many thin because, as a good progressive, his first duty was to establish public order in his Praetorium and in the town itself, and to see to the public hygiene and cleanliness. This of course upset the old bad habits of the townsfolk who do not even know what hygiene is, though they have very clear ideas on the value of the sapek…

This east-west contrast is originally revealed in his collection of portraits: Pius IX, Victor Emmanuel and other eminent people, etc., as well as objects, sacred and profane, which the ex-Minister displays in his apartment.

The official visit of the new Tao-Tâi created a genuine Italian atmosphere, but apart from this it proved an occasion for increasingly closer ties of friendship which will guarantee the serene work of the missionaries in propagating religion in this Italo-Chinese Vicariate.

Hanchungfu, September (?) (sheet 1122)

The Blessing of the Bells in Hanchungfu

It may be very difficult for my gentle readers to form a clear idea of both the enormous distance that separates them from this central part of China called Hanchung, and also the extent of the complications that arise on finding oneself 'interned', owing to the lack of fast and auxiliary means of transport. Before our unstable Young China is in a position to change this state of things and the centuries of slavery, new generations will have to succeed new generations.

So it is no wonder if recently, and thanks to a favourable occasion that was not without incident, that in little more than a six month journey on sea, land and river, three normal sized church bells sent by the renowned firm of Barigozzi & C. in Milan were able to reach us safely in our Hanchungfu. They had been especially commissioned, and not without sacrifice, for the new Cathedral whose erection was completed in these last days by the indefatigable Vicar Apostolic, Monsignor Passerini.

And so a legitimate consolation filled the Italian hearts of the reverend Vicar Apostolic and the missionaries present, as they proceeded to the powerful and deeply moving ritual of the blessing of the bells. It was necessary to conduct this beautiful ceremony behind what might be called 'closed doors' in order to avoid having crowds of curious pagans interrupt the solemnity and mystic exaltation of the ritual, which of course made it no less attractive and was to become a majestic, unforgettable memory for those few who were present.

And now the bells hang up there on that superb bell tower. Its simple line dominates this big pagan town and wins the admiration of all the inhabitants as it rises above the towers and pinnacles of their idolatrous temples, challenging even the town walls which now seem so much smaller in comparison.

Way up there the heart stirring ringing and chiming of the silver voices of these new sacred bronzes, unite with the pure tones of the Catholic missionary announcing to one and all a true peace that is at once sublime and imperishable.

Hanchungfu, undated (sheet 1123)

New Italian Orphanage in Hanchungfu

The latest events in our civil world would disgust anyone of good will and have once again shown us how modern civilisation is garbed in an amalgam that is shamelessly insidious and hostile, much like a raging hydra which rears its seven heads to spew all its poison, vehemently exacerbating against helpless and innocent beings. And why this ferocity? Simply because they wear a religious habit and offer their beneficial support to society. In China, however, in this so-called 'barbarous' land that remains averse to European civilisation by being miserably chained to the soporific grip of paganism, the kindly beneficent feet bringing peace and love of the Sister of Charity, that angel of consolation who, again and again under attack from the Jacobins of Europe, can still freely intercede, with head meekly bowed by sacrifice yet always serenely ready to comfort the groans and sufferings of her brother of a different race and language, and who languishes far from the Life only the Gospel can bestow.

So in our province of southern Shan-Si it is a consolation to confirm the important developments that have occurred in the few years of its life through the charitable and humanitarian works of the 'Culupa' orphanage, which for twenty years has been run with so much love and sacrifice by Italian Canossian nuns.

Hundreds of derelicts, orphans, catechumens, pupils, as well as the aged and abandoned, have been given shelter without drawing distinctions, beneath the succouring wings of Christian charity: all of these can bear unanimous witness to great work the sisters have done in offering divine providence and their beneficent influence, regenerating them to a consciousness of the new morality; and they can thank the mothers and benefactors who have nurtured them in sustenance and education.

The well-defined programme and methods, with which they have set out in different branches along parallel pathways and with the same sense of purpose, are like a fulcrum of all the fertile action upholding the continuous sacrifice of these tireless nuns.

But the essential spirit of these good works knows no goal, and continually tends to spread wherever is heard the groaning of some wretched person and exalts when it can fly to console him with the kiss of peace.

Similarly our Canossians, who have for a long time been looking with love for the possibility of extending elsewhere in this vast territory, in order to carry there their mission of assuagement and education, have finally heard their vows fulfilled. Last March, in the prefectural town of Hanchungfu, under the auspices of the patronage of the Church, suitable provisional premises have been opened for the new Orphanage where the humble Canossian nuns can now begin to undertake their new work with silent enthusiasm and uplifted hearts, making vows that very soon will intensify and bring their beneficent and lasting fruits to the afflictions of the suffering Chinese. Thus they can launch a true civilisation flourishing in the shade of Christian charity.

Gentle reader, may your heart be touched again and again towards these delicate flowers, offered in holocaust for such noble charisma, ever worthy of your friendly admiration, your warmest wishes and your generous help by reminding you that in the centre of faraway China there beats an Italian heart consecrated to mitigating the miseries of others.

Hanchungfu, undated (sheet 114)